Black Seminoles in the Bahamas

UNIVERSITY PRESS OF FLORIDA

Florida A&M University, Tallahassee
Florida Atlantic University, Boca Raton
Florida Gulf Coast University, Ft. Myers
Florida International University, Miami
Florida State University, Tallahassee
New College of Florida, Sarasota
University of Central Florida, Orlando
University of Florida, Gainesville
University of North Florida, Jacksonville
University of South Florida, Tampa
University of West Florida, Pensacola

Black Seminoles in the Bahamas

Rosalyn Howard

University Press of Florida

Gainesville · Tallahassee · Tampa · Boca Raton · Pensacola
Orlando · Miami · Jacksonville · Ft. Myers · Sarasota

First cloth printing, 2002.
First paperback printing, 2008.

27 26 25 24 23   6 5 4 3 2

Library of Congress Cataloging-in-Publication Data
Howard, Rosalyn, 1951–
Black Seminoles in the Bahamas / Rosalyn Howard.
p. cm.
Includes bibliographical references and index.
ISBN 978-0-8130-2559-9 (cloth). ISBN 978-0-8130-2743-2 (ppk)
1. Black Seminoles—Bahamas—Andros Island—History. 2. Black Seminoles—Bahamas—
Andros Island—Government relations. 3. Black Seminoles—Florida—Migrations.
4. African Americans—Florida—Relations with Indians. 5. Andros Island (Bahamas)—
History. 6. Bahamas—Colonization. I. Title.
F1655 .H69 2002
972.96—dc21   20020726333

The University Press of Florida is the scholarly publishing agency for the State University
System of Florida, comprising Florida A&M University, Florida Atlantic University,
Florida Gulf Coast University, Florida International University, Florida State University,
New College of Florida, University of Central Florida, University of Florida, University of
North Florida, University of South Florida, and University of West Florida.

University Press of Florida
2046 NE Waldo Road
Suite 2100
Gainesville, FL 32609
http://upress.ufl.edu

This book is dedicated with love, respect, and gratitude
to my parents, Odessa and Percy, and to my son, Jamil.
They truly are the wind beneath my wings.

Contents

Figures and Maps

Maps

Figures

Acknowledgments

The people of Red Bays welcomed me into their homes and hearts, and for that I will always remain grateful. In particular I want to recognize the invaluable assistance of the Reverend Bertram A. Newton, my primary consultant and friend, who laid the groundwork for the successful completion of this study and who was a powerful source of inspiration. Gertrude Gibson became a valued consultant and friend who gave me shelter in her home, provided me with transportation "up and down de shore," and taught me some important cultural lessons. Many people in Red Bays and other areas where I lived and visited while conducting this research—Nicholls Town, Fresh Creek, the AUTEC Base, Mangrove Cay, San Salvador, Cat Island, Nassau—were integral to the successful completion of this project: Mrs. Omelia Marshall; "Old Iron" Colebrooke; the Reverend Frederick Russell, now deceased; the Reverend Benjamin Lewis; Henry and Jake Wallace; Wilton Russell; Leonora Bain; Ivalene Newton; Deandra Barr; Peggy Barr; Dorothy Colebrooke; the Honorable Dr. Earl D. Deveaux; Brian Cleare; Jessica Minnis; Peter Douglas; Mary Lowe; Father Kirkley Sands; Shelley Bowleg; Dr. Ben Bohl and the staff of the Forfar Field Station; Brenda Borton; the Reverend Captain Tom Sefton and Captain Christie Heath; Freddie Pyfrom; Eris Moncur; Vernamae Knowles; Daisy Jumper; the Bahamas Department of Archives staff: Director Dr. Gail Saunders, Grace Turner, Kim Outten Stubbs, and Sherriley Strachan. The completion of the book was greatly facilitated by the staff of the Faculty Media Center at the University of Central Florida. Special thanks to Angela Greer, Meg Schell, and Sirous Safari.

Friends and colleagues who shared this journey and assisted, inspired, and encouraged me countless times and in various wonderful ways include Noel Ellison, Dr. Faye V. Harrison, Nadine Brown, Dr. Sharon Morrison, Dr. Molefi Asante, Shannell Grimes, Dr. Marvin Haire, Dr. John H. Moore, Dr. Suzanne Phillips, Michele Roquemore Comer, Terry Weik, Deloria "Torchy" Allen, and Dorothy Small.

Introduction

"I never knew that there were Black Seminoles in the Bahamas!" Almost without exception, this is the response I hear each time I tell people about the research that led to the publication of this book. The fact that most people have not heard of Black Seminoles points to a critical void in historical records that is the result of deliberate acts of omission by those who enslaved, colonized, and annihilated millions of African and Native American peoples. Providing the missing pieces to the puzzle of North American history and the African diaspora does not serve the interests of those who wish to perpetuate the notion of the "racial" inferiority of Africans and Native Americans and who continue to use this as justification for their oppression. Recent publications that have significantly contributed to rectifying this void, specifically regarding the Seminoles and Black Seminoles, still make only cursory reference to those who fled to the Bahamas.[1]

This topic has both personal and professional significance to me. As one of the millions of North Americans whose background includes African and Native American ancestry, and whose identity is ascribed as African-American owing to the rule of hypodescent (one drop of "black blood" makes you "black") in the United States, I find it critically important to contribute to a more inclusive perspective of "American" ethnohistory. As an anthropologist, I clearly perceive my responsibility to continue the tradition of the African-American pioneers in anthropology,[2] pushing against the boundaries of inquiry in a discipline largely responsible for establishing and perpetuating the pseudo-scientific constructs of biological "race" that became accepted baselines for erroneous assumptions about the "other" members of humanity.[3]

I "Reach"

My rite of passage into the profession of anthropology commenced in November 1996. I arrived in Red Bays, Andros Island, Bahamas, to begin my one-year residency, toting conscious and subconscious "baggage"—bulging with Westernized, womanist views—that was gradually unpacked over the course of the next year.[4] I felt twinges of guilt whenever I caught myself measuring or judging events and people there by my impalpable, yet omnipresent, cultural yardstick. The following journal entry describes a conversation I had with a Red Bays woman. It illustrates our cultural clash about standing up for oneself when confronted with the demands of others:

> *Journal Entry: May 2, 1997*
>
> *We talk of many things, including her relationships with ——— and others in RB; how they take advantage of her kindness, never thinking of repayment [of money loaned] and how she never stands up to them and demands it. I tell her that she's really not helping them; she's an enabler, helping them to continue their dependency that way. I liken it to a scene where she is stretching out in the street and telling them to run her over—over & over again because she likes it that way. She laughs and says (as she always does when I speak my mind plainly), "Rosslyn, you could talk fool, girl."*

Unlike anthropologist Alan LaFlamme in Green Turtle Cay, another island of the Bahamas, I was warmly welcomed into the Red Bays community.[5] This was, I believe, in part because of my introduction to the community by the Reverend Bertram A. Newton (church pastor, respected community leader, and teacher there for more than forty years), in part because most folks in Red Bays were excited about this opportunity to share their oral history, and in part because of our shared African ancestry. Many of the men there expressed (overtly and covertly) a curiosity about me; consequently, I was viewed suspiciously by many of Red Bays' women because I was single, a novelty, and considered "bright." In the Bahamas, the term *bright* implies a light brown skin tone that is viewed as an asset. This preference for "whiteness" is reinforced when an economically and culturally dominant neighboring country practices it; for the Bahamas this is the United States.[6] Among black Bahamians, as in much of the West Indies and Latin America, degrees of whiteness determine status "in a continuous social-class gradient . . . the lighter the complexion, the greater the economic and social opportunities."[7]

Another label attached to me was "American." This was a rather unusual experience for me, having grown up in the United States, where the black-white binary racial paradigm, persistent racism, and my brown skin color have brought into question the validity of my identity as an "authentic American." Now, here, in the Bahamas—a country where people of African descent are 85 percent of the total population, I am living in Red Bays whose population is predominantly people of African descent, with a pinch of Seminole ancestry in the mix. Yet I am once again set apart, distinguished this time in a "positive" way because of the *shade* of my skin color, perhaps owing to the legacy of hierarchical colonial structure and a pattern of neocolonialism. Despite my being initially suspected as a "DEA [Drug Enforcement Agency] agent," my work among Red Bayans progressed relatively rather smoothly. Most residents in the settlement were eventually convinced that I was not an agent of the DEA, and, equally important, not rich (a widely held stereotype about Americans in this tourist-driven economy). I remained, however, very much an enigma in Red Bays as a woman visiting, of my own volition, a foreign country without a man in tow. I was constantly queried by the men of Red Bays: "Your man let you come all the way down here *alone*?!" They found it incomprehensible that neither did I have—nor did I feel the need to have—the explicit permission of a husband or significant other to be working there.

Situating My "Self"

The subjective effects inherent in qualitative research can never be eliminated, but they can be addressed by acknowledging the power relationships that are based upon race, class, gender, and knowledge, and by affirming the ways that these relationships affect the research environment.[8] This approach encourages an investigation of the social relationship between myself and the respondents and situates me within the research process. As revealed in the following journal entry, I was keenly aware of all these issues with respect to my position, reception, and perception in the settlement. As an educated, "bright," independent, American woman, I automatically achieved a status in the settlement unattainable for any other woman there.

Journal Entry: February 12, 1997

Thoughts on Fieldwork: Here, on the edge of pineyards and sea, I am looked upon by men and women as an enigma. Feared (resented?) by men because I am an example of female latitude (independence) they do not wish their women to glimpse . . . perhaps. Gossiped about by women ("who is that 'bright' American woman?") who eye me suspiciously as I talk with their men, and their female "enemies" in the settlement. Will they trust me when I come talk to them, after seeing me talking to "her/him"? Coerced by children to supply them with money or candy . . . after all, I'm sure they believe, if I am from the U.S. I must be rich! Weary under the pressure of multiple expectations from home, school and here. Yet I rise when "day clean," prepared to make each day meaningful. After all . . . I cannot stand outside my skin as the "observer." This is not only my "fieldwork." This is my life!

I vividly recall this day and am struck by the realization that participant observation is definitely not a neutral task. Texts on the nature of fieldwork that I perused before embarking upon this journey had, of course, attested to this fact, but the words just did not penetrate my psyche until I was here, in the thick of it. Using the "spyglass of anthropology,"[9] I aimed to pinpoint, elaborate, and analyze their culture, and their lived experience, experience that did not always take place at a conscious level.[10] Sometimes this process felt artificial, or invasive. I realized that not only was I impacting their lives, but they mine.

The following ethnohistorical account is offered with full acknowledgment of my own biases and filters. I have grappled with my subjective presence and am satisfied that my rendering is "how I saw it."[11] In her autobiography, *Dust Tracks on a Road,* anthropologist Zora Neale Hurston gives voice to my feelings so much more eloquently: "Nothing that God ever made is the same thing to more than one person. That is natural. There is no single face in nature, because every eye that looks upon it, sees it from its own angle. So every man's spice box seasons his own food. Naturally, I picked up the reflections of life around me with my own instruments, and absorbed what I gathered according to my inside juices."[12]

My mission—to address the historical, structural amnesia that obscures African and indigenous peoples' interactions and negates their integral roles in the historiography of the Americas and the Caribbean (the "New World") —begins in chapter 1 with an explication of this history and an exploration of how the slave trade transformed the landscape of North America. The trade became one vehicle for significant interactions between indigenous and African peoples there, interactions that some scholars estimate may have originated—voluntarily—thousands of years ago. Details about the relationships formed between the Seminole Indians and Africans in the southeastern territory of what later became the United States are the subject of chapter 2.

Another aspect of my mission is to present for the first time an in-depth rendering of the essence of social memory that sustains the Black Seminole heritage of Red Bays. In chapter 3, Black Seminole descendants relate the stories passed down to them by their parents, grandparents, and great-grandparents about the initial journey to the Bahamas. Chapter 4 contextualizes their presence in the historical and contemporary Bahamas. Chapter 5 brings to life the contemporary community of Red Bays, Andros Island, where the descendants of many of the original refugees currently reside. The concept of cultural identity in general, and their personal perceptions about it, is explored in chapter 6. Chapter 7 presents an overview of the Black Seminole diaspora—contrasting the consequences of eastward versus westward migration—and describes recent encounters and planned events designed to establish relations between the Seminole Tribe of Florida and the Bahamian Black Seminole descendants.

This book probes into one layer of what is a deep and rich history and, hopefully, provides a point of departure for future research into the many unwritten stories of African and Native American encounters in the New World.

A Brief Explanation of Terminology

I use the terms *African* or *black* to refer to persons who were brought to the Americas from Africa and enslaved. Their descendants who were born in the Americas are alternately referred to as *creole, African-American,* or *black.* The terms *indigenous* and *Native American* are used interchangeably throughout the text to refer to peoples who were the original inhabitants of North America. The terms *Euroamerican* and *white* refer to persons whose predominant ancestry is European or whose identities have been socially constructed as such, and who are elsewhere referred to as *Americans.* Controversies surround the use of all of these terms, but a comprehensive discussion of this important subject is beyond the scope of this project.

One of the longest unwritten chapters
in the history of the United States is
that treating of the relations of the
Negroes and the Indians.

Carter G. Woodson

1 ᨐᨑ

The Significance of African and Indigenous Peoples' Contacts in the Americas

The condition of invisibility for Americans of African descent, so poignantly examined by author Ralph Ellison in his novel *Invisible Man,* is reiterated by the position in which African and indigenous peoples are traditionally situated in the canon of world history. The historical record of the Americas and the Caribbean—or the "New World"—suffers from the chronic malaise of structural amnesia, a Eurocentric process by which "those events which have little relevance to the structure of . . . white society are relegated to historical oblivion."[1] Information regarding the profound and diverse historical relationships forged between indigenous peoples and Africans in the Americas has been systematically omitted or consigned to an obscure footnote.[2] This process, which consistently relates historical events from the oppositional perspective of Europeans and the "Other," is a form of hegemony—a two-pronged method of social domination and control, based on force/violence and/or consent/education.[3] This book counters the hegemonic project by explicating the relationship of two particular groups of neglected peoples, traditionally subsumed under the category of "Other"—the Seminole Indians of Florida and the Africans who sought refuge among them after escaping enslavement on North American plantations.

When Europeans embarked on their destructive path of colonization and imperialism, they not only colonized the physical world, "they colonized information about the world."[4] Since knowledge is socially and intellectually negotiated, the exclusion of vital information results in a knowledge base that is suspect. The exclusion of colonized peoples' histories is fundamental to dehumanization and legitimizes their treatment as inferior beings; "a people with no history worth mentioning . . . have no humanity worth defending."[5]

During the holocaust of European colonialism, indigenous peoples and Africans suffered and endured under the forces of domination, racism, oppression, and genocide in the New World. Over the course of four hundred years of European contact, the indigenous population of North America was devastated, shrinking from an estimated ten million in 1492 to less than one million.[6] Demographic devastation also befell the indigenous peoples of the Caribbean region—the Caribs, Lucayans, and Arawaks. Their demise was achieved by various measures, including overwork, genocide, and exposure to epidemic and epizootic diseases.[7]

Familiarity with the environment permitted a small advantage for indigenous peoples in North America in their efforts to resist enslavement and death. If caught, however, runaways were often exported to the West Indies where their escape would be more difficult. Two events figured prominently in the fate of indigenous peoples. First, in 1542 Spain outlawed their ownership as "property," and second, the colonial American assembly outlawed their enslavement in 1679. Africans became the one remaining abundant source of cheap labor that could meet the needs of the colonizers.[8]

Africans had a lower but still significant mortality rate, suffering the loss of a conservatively estimated 20 percent of the ten to twenty million people who involuntarily left the African continent and perished either during the Middle Passage or after enslavement in the New World.[9]

The relative neglect of scholarly attention to the dynamic of contact between the survivors of this holocaust not only creates an impression of their impotency as agents in the genesis of New World societies, but also buttresses the hierarchy that places European society and culture at the apex of so-called civilization. The study of African and indigenous peoples' interactions illuminates their important roles in the evolution of New World cultures.

The Political Economy of Slavery in North America

While there were substantial geopolitical differences in the nature of enslavement, the process was, pragmatically, a dynamic continuum of domination and oppression by which the English, Spanish, Dutch, French, and Portuguese exploited Africans and indigenous peoples in the New World. In North America the British, French, and Spanish alternately vied for control of various territories. The British, however, were to play the most influential role.

Clearly, the major objective of the Europeans who descended upon the Americas was personal and national profit. Incredible fortunes were made from the uncompensated labor of enslaved Africans and indigenous peoples. An estimated thirty thousand Africans were enslaved in North America by 1715.[10] Over the next century, this number rose to over a half million, peaking between 1780 and 1810. The network of powerful people who sanctioned and profited from the slave trade included: the clergymen who blessed it; the British Crown and its colonial agents in Boston and Williamsburg; African leaders; merchants in Newport, Rhode Island, and Liverpool, England; Charleston traders; Virginia planters; lawyers and judges; and agents who insured the human "cargoes" during the Middle Passage.[11] The doctrine of Manifest Destiny justified European territorial expansion in North America and reinforced the ideology of racial superiority.

Maintenance of Euroamerican hegemony required elevating slavery from a de facto to a de jure institution. The legal institutionalization of African bondage in colonial North America laid the economic foundation for Euroamerican prosperity both in the North and the South of what became the United States of America. The requirements for achieving prosperity differed in the North versus the South. In the South, slavery functioned both as an economic institution and a system of social control for thousands of indigenous and African peoples. In many instances, Euroamericans in the South were demographic minorities, and the institution of slave codes—justified by the idea of inferior "races" or racialization—significantly increased their power to suppress and oppress despite being significantly outnumbered. Although slavery certainly existed in the North, the overall requirements of industry there dictated the need for a different type of labor force. Northerners, however, did reap financial and social benefits from the "peculiar institution" prevalent in the South. Contrary to the belief that the ethical dilemma of human enslavement led to the abolition movement, Northern society had instead reached the point where the financial liabilities of slavocracy outweighed the benefits. It was only then that one heard sonorous calls for abolition.[12]

Labor Needs on the New Frontier

The taming of the New World frontier and the spread of the plantation system in the Americas and the Caribbean required a substantial amount of labor, more than the colonists were capable of or inclined to perform themselves. The serious need for labor did not, however, induce the colonists to enslave other Europeans; indentured servitude with a specific term limitation of four to seven years was typically the closest European immigrants ever came to bondage. Another variant of this status for European immigrant laborers, usually Germans or Swiss, was that of redemptioner: "A redemptioner, unlike an indentured servant, was often able to pay a part of the cost of passage [to the United States]. Merchants took whatever money the redemptioner had and provided him and his family with passage aboard ship and a contract to deliver them to America. The redemptioner was usually allowed fourteen days to try to secure the balance due; if he could not, he was sold into indentured servitude for a length of time roughly equivalent to the amount of money due the captain."[13]

Many of those immigrants were women and men who chose the option of indentured servitude over imprisonment or death sentences in England.[14] Others were victims of unscrupulous ship owners who conspired with judges to convict innocent people and subsequently sell them into indentureships, a process whereby "a whole hierarchy from courtly secretaries and grave judges down to the jailers and turnkeys . . . insisted on having a share in the spoils. . . . The leading merchants and public officials were all involved in the practice."[15]

Virginia colonists purportedly used the term "servants" to describe the first Africans to disembark from a Dutch ship in North America. As free persons of color, their status was considered that of indenture rather than enslavement. This interpretation of status is ambiguous and controversial because English-language usage in the 1600s defined "slave" as a category of servant. Therefore, the use of the word *servant* in documents such as the Virginia censuses of 1623 and 1624 "in no way denied the slave status of Africans . . . [who] had no contracts for service, and for sure they had not entered service voluntarily. . . . An indentured servants' contract and, thus, labor was salable, but the person was not. Slavery was heritable, and no other personal labor obligation was. Africans alone were marked from birth as slave labor."[16] Heritability was matrilineal, so regardless of the father's status, a person joined the ranks of the enslaved if his or her mother was enslaved.[17]

The colonial legislature made periodic attempts to limit the slave trade in an attempt to curb the escalating demographic imbalance in some regions. Occasionally motivated by ethics, they had as their primary inducement to intercede in the trade the fear of revolts by the enslaved, the threat of which grew as the ratio of Africans to European Americans grew in favor of the Africans. Such was the case in the Carolinas.

The Carolinas

Plantation owners who transported enslaved Africans and their system of slavery from Barbados were a major factor in establishing the colony of Carolina in the 1660s. These settlers made no pretense about their motivations; African enslavement was integral to their development plans for the colony. By 1720, 70 percent of the population of Carolina was Africans and creoles, their American-born descendants; the majority was located in the southern part of the colony.[18] The dramatic imbalance between the number of Africans and Europeans aroused deep concern and fear among Carolina colonists. Carolina separated into two states—North and South Carolina—in 1729, and by 1790 the African/European ratio was reduced to 50 percent through limitations imposed on importation and by an increased recruitment of white settlers to the area. However, when importation restrictions threatened profits and socioeconomic status, the trade resumed.

South Carolina's semitropical climate was conducive to the production of two of the most profitable crops grown in North America—cotton and rice. It was rice, however, that was destined to become the foundation of colonial South Carolina's economy. Because the English colonizers had no aptitude for rice production, slave traders for the South Carolina low country targeted African laborers from specific regions of Africa; the most highly valued were, naturally, people from the rice-growing regions of West Africa. Rice cultivation dated back to circa 1500 B.C. along the West African coast. Africans from this region, therefore, tended to be highly skilled in growing rice and were favored by South Carolina planters, who willingly paid higher prices for them.[19] A person's "property value" at point of sale in Africa, as well as upon arrival at the North American auction house, was based upon such assessments of skills and attributes.[20]

Despite a preference for Senegambians (people from the area known as the Rice Coast), South Carolinian planters eventually imported greater numbers of Africans from Angola owing to their increased availability. From 1735 to 1740, approximately 70 percent of South Carolina's slave labor emanated from the Congo and Angola regions. The planting and harvesting methods used were strikingly similar to those practiced in Africa. Bountiful rice crops generated substantial profits, affording plantation owners the highest per capita income in the colonies by the mid eighteenth century, and they enjoyed a powerful lobby in the government that bargained for troops to control the large enslaved population. The advent of war with England, however, refocused Northerners' priorities; no longer would troops be sent to reinforce the slavocracy, nor could South Carolinians adequately support the war effort by deploying their own limited number of troops. Southern plantation owners had grown accustomed to aid from the colonial government when confronting crises with runaways and revolts. This policy change allowed many Africans to make their escape to British battle lines and to enlist in the fight against the Euroamericans, in exchange for freedom. Runaways were an important factor for the British, and many of them left North America with their British allies after their defeat.[21]

The influence of this powerful rice aristocracy remained strong, however, and later championed South Carolina's secession from the Union, an act that helped to precipitate the Civil War.[22]

Resistance and Maroon Communities

The English term *maroon* is derived from the Spanish word *cimarrón*. The term originally referred to domestic cattle that escaped into the hills of Hispaniola (currently Haiti and the Dominican Republic). The term was later applied to indigenous and African peoples who escaped European enslavers and established separate communities; the term "had strong connotations of 'fierceness,' of being 'wild' and 'unbroken.'"[23]

Forming maroon communities was one of many resistance strategies employed by the enslaved. Herbert Aptheker, who documented numerous examples of maroons in the antebellum South, describes marronage as the expression of resistance on the part of the "outraged victims" of American slavery.[24] While the majority of these were established in the New World by African and creole runaways—who fought against indigenous peoples as well as Europeans and Euroamericans—others were formed as alliances of Africans and indigenous peoples, united in their resistance of Euroamerican aggression.[25]

Petit marronage—characterized as "repetitive or periodic truancy with temporary goals such as visiting a relative or a lover on a neighboring plantation"[26]—was frequently tolerated. Marronage on a large scale, however—such as what occurred in Brazil, Colombia, Cuba, Ecuador, Hispaniola, Jamaica, Mexico, and Surinam—drew their ire. Maroon settlements of African runaways in the Blue Mountains of Jamaica and those of the "Bush Negroes" and Saramaka in the jungles of Guyana and Surinam respectively claimed some very intriguing names: "God Knows Me and None Else," "Disturb Me If You Dare," "Come Try Me If You Be Men," and "I Shall Moulder before I Shall Be Taken."[27] The greatest maroon community, lasting for almost a hundred years (1600–94), was the Republic of Palmares in northeastern Brazil, ruled by Ganga-Zumba, whose name combines the Angolan word for "great" and the Tupi Indian word for "ruler."[28]

Marronage in North America did exist, but on a much smaller scale. Fifty or more of these communities existed from 1672 to 1864 in the less accessible areas of South Carolina, North Carolina, Virginia, Louisiana, Florida, Georgia, Mississippi, and Alabama.[29] The terrain of these states offered relatively good hiding places in mountainous areas, swamps, and forests, but not nearly as formidable as the mountains and jungles of Jamaica and South America. Dismal Swamp, the most notorious maroon community in the United States, was located between Virginia and North Carolina. The population there approximated two thousand, and trade was conducted with Euroamericans on the periphery of the swamp.[30] Maroons employed any and all means to ensure their survival, enlisting knowledge gleaned from indigenous, African, and plantation cultures.[31]

The dearth of maroon communities established in North America (in contrast to their success in South America and the Caribbean) was primarily due to climate and geography, not degree of initiative by the enslaved. Spanish Florida presented the best locale for a viable North American maroon community. Its swampy terrain, as well as the presence of amicable indigenous peoples and Spanish officials, proved conducive to long-term refuge for formerly enslaved Africans. Some Africans who escaped the plantations chose sanctuary among the Spanish, at Fort Mose, the first legally sanctioned black community in North America, located approximately two miles from St. Augustine. Archaeological evidence suggests that the most successful maroon community for Black Seminoles in Florida was at Peliklakaha. More details on these communities of escaped Africans follow in the next chapter.

2 ༚

New Identities, New Alliances

To ensure their domination, the Euroamericans used not only force and violence but also a system of justifications, stereotypes, and psychosocial indoctrination. Dogma such as the excellence of whiteness and the aesthetic degradation of blackness formed one of the psychological pillars of exploitation.[1] The era in which Euroamericans heightened their assault on the Seminoles in Florida was one where claims of the natural inferiority of indigenous and African peoples acquired new theoretical and scientific authority. Racialization achieved an unprecedented level of credence in the mid nineteenth century based upon pseudoscientific "evidence" that posited a natural hierarchy of "races." Spencer's "survival of the fittest" philosophy and his "scientifically grounded" premise that equated "black" with evil or savage reinforced the popularly held belief in the superiority of European "races" and cultures. "These themes were subsequently reproduced in the mass media as science, integrated into domestic and foreign policy, and appropriated by white supremacist demagogues."[2]

The concept of a superior "white" race was the common denominator used to subvert socioeconomic inequities among the Euroamerican classes. Construction of this new "white" identity provided racial privileges for Euroamerican immigrants—many of whom had been impoverished or imprisoned in England—that elevated them above enslaved Africans, although there may not have been much contrast in their actual life circumstances. Their lower wages and socioeconomic status were augmented by the "public and psychological wage" associated with whiteness.[3] The veil of contentment lifted, however, as Euroamerican immigrants "realized that Negroes were part of a group of millions of workers who were enslaved by law, and whose competition kept white labor out of the work of the South and threatened its wages and stability in the North."[4] Poor, propertyless Euroamericans, often employed as indentured servants, shared African and indigenous peoples' exclusion from the Declaration of Independence's pronouncement that "all men are created equal."

Ethnogenesis: Fluid Identities in the New World

Cultural identity is a result of socialization, much as religion, sexism, and racism.[5] Always "in process," the construction of cultural identity is dynamic and contingent upon the variables of situation, individual interpretation, and power. Socioeconomic forces, political exigencies, new experiences, and life cycle changes, in turn, modify these variables.[6] Accordingly, cultural identity among the Black Seminoles and the Seminole Indians evolved, adapting in a context of rapidly changing historical processes and situational forces. From their ethnogenesis,[7] these unique New World ethnic groups were involved in processes of identity formation and re-formation. Both of these groups were not monolithic, but were aggregations of many ethnicities, tribes,[8] and nations; various Indian nations comprised the Seminoles, and, likewise, Africans from many different ethnic groups and nations comprised the Black Seminoles. Their acculturative experiences should be differentiated from the processes of creolization and transculturation, terms that connote a synthesis of cultures to greater or lesser degrees between members of groups in contact. Ethnogenesis, instead, describes an internal group process wherein a new ethnic identity is created in response to conflict, domination, and resistance.[9] Such was the case for Seminoles and Black Seminoles. Self-redefinition and cultural adaptation was a consequence of forces such as demographic collapse, forced relocation, enslavement, ethnocide, and genocide.

Ethnogenesis of the Seminole People

Seminole culture is derived from an amalgamation of linguistically and culturally diverse indigenous nations, a familiar scenario for them, since the Muskogees, from whom the Seminoles emerged, had always been heterogeneous. Muskogee constituents emanated from many different nations of indigenous peoples in the North American territories now known as Georgia and Alabama. Notwithstanding these peoples' cultural and linguistic diversity, English traders arbitrarily conflated these nations under the classification "Creek."[10] The etymology of the term has been alternately attributed to the proximity of these peoples to numerous rivers and streams, and to their having resided along the Ochesee Creek. When remnants of the Creek Confederacy moved into Florida territory, beginning early in the eighteenth century, this heterogeneity was further diversified by the integration of indigenous nations already residing there.

The Creek Confederacy, also known as the Muskogee Polity, was split into two major groups, situated alongside two watersheds: the Upper Creeks along the Coosa and Tallapoosa Rivers in Alabama, and the Lower Creeks near the Chattahoochee and Flint Rivers in Georgia. The Muskogee Polity incorporated a variety of ethnic groups: the Hitchiti-speaking groups, including the Apalachicolas, Chiahas, Hitchitis, Yamasees, and others; the Alabamas, including the Alabamas, Koasatis, Tuskegees, and others; and the Muskogees, including the Kasihtas, Cowetas, Coosas, Abihkas, Hothliwahalis, Eufaulas, Hilibis, Wakokais, Tuckabahchees, Okchais, and others.[11] Explorer William Bartram interprets the Upper Creek and Lower Creek designations differently; he assigns the "Creeks proper [to the category of 'Upper Creeks'], while his 'Lower Creeks' are the Seminole."[12] In addition to the above groups, the Yuchis (Euchees), Shawnees, Natchezes, Coushattas, Choctaws, Cherokees, and African-American Freedmen have at various times been considered part of the Creek and Seminole Nations.[13]

Muskogee towns and chiefdoms were modified and realigned owing both to the influence of Euroamerican—French, English and Spanish—incursions into indigenous territories, and to alliances formed with the Euroamericans by various indigenous factions. The primary town in the Muskogee chiefdom was Coweta. The dominance of the Cowetas (their chief being known as the "emperor" of the Creeks, according to the Spaniards and the French) allowed them to incorporate other chiefdoms by persuasion or force, demanding conformity

to the Coweta language and ceremonial practices.[14] Recalcitrants, mainly derived from the incorporated ethnic groups who objected to Creek alliances with
the Europeans, seceded from the Muskogees and were important factors in the
ethnogenesis of the Seminole nation in Florida.[15]

One of the primary dissidents was Seacoffee (Seepeycoffee), son of the
micco (king or chief), of the Coweta. Seacoffee led a migration from British-
controlled Georgia and Alabama to Spanish-controlled Florida in the 1720s
and 1730s. He "understood the strategic and geopolitical importance of securing a fighting base in this sparsely populated peninsula where, in league
with other Native American and black allies, the chances of survival could be
greatly enhanced."[16] There they established the nascent Seminole chiefdom in
the region of present-day Tallahassee.[17] Beginning ten years later, after the Yamassee War,[18] the Oconees—another ethnic group associated with the Muskogees—led by Wakapuchasee (Cowkeeper) moved onto the Alachua Prairie, an
area now known as Gainesville, where, some suggest, they became the first
group to be labeled "Seminoles." The Oconees conquered various groups during their expansion southward, including the Yamassees,[19] and eventually
dominated the Seminole nation, retaining power through matrilineal succes-
sion until the late nineteenth century.[20]

The Etymology of "Seminole"

There are many different theories on the derivation of the term *Seminole*. In the
Muskogee language, *Seminole* or *Simanóli* means "runaways."[21] Some scholars
claim that the Creeks first used this term when referring to "Afro-American
runaways"[22] who had escaped enslavement in Georgia and the Carolinas, and
who subsequently settled in Florida. Congressman Joshua Giddings alternately
refers to the self-liberated Africans who escaped as "Seminoles," "Exiles," and
"Negro Indians."[23] Others concur that *Seminole* means "wild" or "runaway," but
argue instead that the name applies to Creeks who abandoned their territories
in Alabama and Georgia and settled in Florida.[24] *Seminole* is further speculated
to be ultimately derived from the Spanish *cimarrón* or *cimarrone,* meaning
"wild one." Sturtevant suggests that the meaning of *Seminole* evolved into use
as "the ethnonym for all Florida Indians; and it was the specific ethnonym for
the band derived ultimately from Alachua, as opposed to other bands called
Miccosukee, Creek, Tallahassee, Yuchi, Hitchiti, Spanish Indians."[25]

Littlefield (1977) concurs with this point, asserting that *Seminole* was used in the 1770s to refer to the Alachua band of Lower Creeks and that by the 1820s the term referred to Lower Creeks and Upper Creeks and Yuchis who had migrated to and settled in Florida. Wright (1986), conversely, claims that some Creeks distinguished themselves as Seminoles before going to Florida. Most other scholars suggest, however, that use of the designation *Seminole* originated only when members of the Lower Creeks and Upper Creeks (as well as remnants from other indigenous groups) left the settled Creek towns in Alabama and Georgia and migrated to Florida from the seventeenth to the early nineteenth centuries.

Northern Florida's growth stemmed from intermittent waves of Creeks and other indigenous immigrants. Early Creek migrations encountered several indigenous groups: the Apalachees in the west; the Timucuas in the north; the Calusas in the south. Diseases imported by Europeans and slaving raids by Carolinians had decimated indigenous Floridians' ranks. The Creek War of 1813–14 precipitated the final significant migration that effectively doubled the indigenous population in Florida.[26] Geopolitical competition among the French, British, and Spanish intensified in the region as these international actors vied for favored status with the Seminoles, from whom they sought to secure land or gain influence. The Europeans' persuasive arsenal included conferring dubious honors upon indigenous leaders, such as European titles and military commissions.[27]

African Runaways: Georgia and the Carolinas

Proximity to Florida, familiarity with their environs, and large tracts of unsettled land in the southeastern United States provided ripe conditions for Africans' escape from Georgian and Carolinian plantations. Additionally, the state of confusion that ensued during the French and American Revolutions provided a serendipitous diversion that facilitated their flight.[28] Many sought refuge among various indigenous groups. The proffer of sanctuary extended by the Spanish in Florida, however, must have been one of the strongest motivators for Africans to embark on the dangerous journey toward freedom.

A 1693 Royal Spanish decree promised protection to all enslaved who reached St. Augustine on the condition that they adopt the Roman Catholic religion. Africans who had been enslaved on the plantations of southeastern

North America, especially in the neighboring Carolinas and Georgia, eagerly sought a new life of freedom in Spanish Florida. Plantation owners' aristocratic, antibourgeois, and paternalistic attitudes may have clouded their awareness of the enslaved's aspirations for freedom, perceiving them as "happy" in perpetual servitude. Their naïveté would increase their vulnerability to deception, which certainly worked to the advantage of the enslaved peoples.

The Spanish granted newly freed Africans plots of land two miles north of St. Augustine, where they established the first legally sanctioned black community in North America: Gracia Réal de Santa Terésa de Mosé, also known as Fort Mose.[29] The motives for this invitation from Spanish officials were not as altruistic as may be believed. Greater than their concern for the souls of these poor Africans, or respect for their humanity, was the Spaniards' urgent need for them as "buffers" against invasions by United States residents and troops. By offering formerly enslaved Africans sanctuary, they could undermine the stability of the emergent plantation system that threatened their existence.

The Seminoles were also protected under Spanish law and were guaranteed land and property rights. These property rights extended also to Africans, or Black Seminoles, living among them who were considered to be their "slaves." However, Spanish law also granted limited rights and legal protection that were absent in other systems of enslavement.[30]

Indigenous and African Peoples' Alliances

Sociopolitical alliances between Africans and indigenous peoples were the source of great fear among Euroamericans and Europeans, who fiercely sought to prevent them unless these alliances were to their advantage, as was the case when the Spanish used them as a buffer zone against Euroamericans invading Florida. In order to effect fragmentation, Euroamericans fanned the flames of animosity by (1) paying indigenous peoples to recapture Africans;[31] (2) arming slaves and setting them to attack indigenous villages, often under false pretenses; and (3) inciting indigenous peoples by blaming Africans for epidemics that ravaged many indigenous villages but were actually perpetrated by Europeans. Both Euroamericans and Europeans effectively utilized their superior military force and material wealth to foment divisiveness between African and indigenous peoples, creating a "Hobbesian war of 'all against all' in which strategic considerations of military power, and economic forces of material profit, more often than not outweighed crosscutting ties based on resistance to domination."[32] The relationship of most Seminole Indians and African runaways was an important exception to this scenario.

Together the Seminoles and Africans represented a formidable obstacle to Euroamerican incursions into East Florida, prompting Governor Mitchell to complain that the Spanish "governour has proclaimed freedom to every Negro who will join his standard. . . . Indeed the principal strength of the garrison at St. Augustine consists of Negroes."[33] Their ancillary role continued until 1813.

Africans and Seminoles formed alliances to combat aggressors because of their mutual interest in securing the Florida territory as a haven for themselves.[34] While this broader goal was mutual, the details were individually specific: Seminole Indians fought to retain their land and livelihood, while Africans fought against a return to enslavement, or death at the hands of bounty-hunting Coweta Indians and angry slaveowners wishing to make an example of them.

The majority of Africans who escaped into Florida were creoles, persons born in the United States. They significantly eclipsed the percentage of Africa-born—designated "new Negroes" (or "salt-water Negroes")—and males sharply outnumbered female runaways. Having lived for some time on the plantations before their escape, many of the formerly enslaved Africans had become familiar with the culture of Euroamericans and could predict their behavior in certain instances.[35] Some runaways were experienced seamen who would boldly hire on as crew on ships that sailed from Carolina and Georgia ports, under the pretense that they were "free" men. Artisans represented a large fraction of those who effectively made the journey to freedom. They were in demand, especially coopers, and were frequently hired out by their masters to work in urban areas of South Carolina in exchange for a certain portion of their profit. Ironically, their specialized abilities had served to strengthen the rationale for their enslavement. Permission to hire out also meant an increase in status and "gave talented slaves both a sense of self-esteem and a certain measure of freedom from supervision, which enabled them to make their work patterns more tolerable, and even occasionally glorious parts of a meaningful culture, however artificially constricted it may have been."[36]

This clever blending of accommodation and resistance allowed the enslaved a tenuous "freedom" that may have in some measure mitigated the exigencies of involuntary servitude. Some used the money earned to purchase freedom for themselves or relatives. Others used their sanctioned independence as an opportunity for escape. Because it was not unusual to see these skilled artisans traveling about town on various jobs or errands, they did not attract as much suspicion as other enslaved people plotting escape. Plantation owner James Bulloch advertised in the July 13, 1768, *Georgia Gazette* for just such a runaway: "a Negroe fellow called Cato, a cooper by trade, and well known in Savannah, and his wife July, a washerwoman, had a written license from the subscriber to come to town, and there to work for a month from the 13th of June last, but have not been seen or heard of since."

Georgia newspapers also carried advertisements from slaveowners in the Carolinas and even Florida seeking the return of their "property."[37] A December 1783 runaway-ad describes a man as "by trade a carpenter, of a yellowish complexion well-known in and about Savannah; he went away in a new paddling cypress canoe...and carried with him a broad axe, a handsaw, and several other carpenter tools, by which it is supposed he intends to pass as a free fellow, or as having my permission to work out."

The detail with which runaways were described ranged widely, and many ads contained very intriguing details. For example: "Will, a cooper, remarkable for being covered from his waist downwards with the marks of a severe correction given him in the West Indies for an attempt to murder, is subject to fits on the full and change of the moon"; "two of his upper fore teeth are filed sharp"; "a Negroe wench, named Esther, branded on the breast *J. Bowman*"; "Long Hercules, otherwise called Doctor Hercules, from his remarkable conjurations of pigs feet, rattlesnakes teeth, and from the feet and legs of several sick people, many of whom still believe him in reality to have performed miracles."[38]

Emergent Alliances

Scrutiny of the nexus of Seminoles and Africans in Florida reveals a unique relationship unparalleled by those formed between other indigenous peoples and Africans in North America. This fact has been systematically ignored in most traditional historical accounts of the southeastern territory of the United States. The principal indigenous nations in the southeastern United States were the Cherokees, Choctaws, Chickasaws, Creeks, and Seminoles. Together they constituted the "Five Civilized Tribes," a designation assigned them by Europeans because of the relatively cooperative relationships they enjoyed with these groups as opposed to other indigenous nations.[39] With the exception of the Seminoles, all of these nations became large slaveholders as early as 1748.[40] The character of the institution of slavery among these nations may be ranked hierarchically: the Cherokees, the most acculturated of all the nations, aligned themselves with Euroamerican-style chattel slavery; the Chickasaws and Choctaws were noted both for their cruelty to the enslaved and as "great sticklers for racial purity"; the Creeks, ranked as less "civilized" than the former nations, practiced a patriarchal attitude toward the enslaved. Runaway Africans were nowhere better received than among the Seminoles, with whom they lived in relative freedom in Florida.[41]

Euroamericans were incensed about the Seminole system of so-called slavery that more closely resembled tenant farming than chattel slavery. In the 1820s, an estimated four hundred Africans lived among the Seminoles and appeared to outsiders as "wholly independent, or at least regardless of the authority of their masters, and are slaves but in name."[42] In 1826 Governor DuVal admonished the Seminoles, "You are not to mind what the Negroes say: they will lie and lead you astray, in the hope to escape from their white owners, and that you will give them refuge and hide them. Do your duty and give them up. They care nothing for you, further than to make use of you, to keep out of the hands of their masters.... Deliver them up, rid your nation of a serious pest, and do what, as honest men, you should not hesitate to do; then your white brothers will say you have done them justice, like honest, good men."[43]

The principal goal of the Euroamerican plot to annex Florida was to eliminate the significant threat to the institution of slavery posed by Spanish-controlled Florida. The displacement and relocation of the Seminoles, both in Florida and Indian Territory, had much to do with their possession of "black slaves."[44]

Ethnogenesis of the Black Seminoles

Like the Seminoles, African peoples who were forcibly removed from their homelands were not a homogeneous group. They originated from geographically and culturally diverse areas of West and Central Africa. Even those who originated from the same geographic area did not necessarily share cultural identities, as Terence Ranger comments: "Almost all recent studies of nineteenth-century pre-colonial Africa have emphasized that far from there being a single 'tribal' identity, most Africans moved in and out of multiple identities, defining themselves at one moment as subject to this chief, at another moment as a member of that cult, at another moment part of this clan, and at yet another moment as an initiate in that professional guild."[45]

The illusory concept of "bounded groups" was actually invented by Europeans as a means to effectively control Africans. They achieved hegemony by arbitrarily codifying fluid identities into bounded tribal systems.[46] African social systems cannot adequately be analyzed using the Western paradigm of bounded identity because, prior to colonization, they claimed multiple identities across geopolitical and sociocultural boundaries.

Diverse African peoples, violently thrust together in the New World, were confronted with the necessity of reconstructing individual and group identities; the common denominator was their subjective position of "slave." Cultural and social memories were interpolated with varied oppressive social forces to which they were subjected. "Temporary attachments" in the form of fictive kin groups had their genesis under the dynamic circumstances of enslavement and served as catalysts in the transformation of identities.[47] Family stability was impossible in the North American variant of slavery:[48] families were disassembled at the whim of the master; husbands and wives, parents and children were sold capriciously to different buyers.

The Africans who forged alliances with the Seminoles became, in many ways, "an integral part of the Seminole people."[49] Enslaved Africans who fled into Florida, and subsequently became known as Black Seminoles, did not, however, automatically become culturally Indian.

Africans, in many cases, adopted the Seminole style of dress and mode of dwelling construction. However, archaeological excavations and travelers' accounts suggest that Black Seminoles most often lived in separate communities, usually located nearby their Seminole "masters."[50] There they were permitted a substantial degree of autonomy in exchange for payment of a percentage of their harvest to the Seminole chief. Confirmation of this is also provided in the account of an American doctor, William Haynes Simmons: "The Negroes dwell in towns apart from the Indians, and are the finest looking people I have ever seen. They dress and live pretty much like the Indians, each having a gun, and hunting a portion of his time. Like the Indians, they plant in common, and form an *Indian field apart*, which they attend together."[51]

The "Indian field apart" is an area of cultivated land "whose produce was consigned to the Seminole micco who ruled the town."[52] This physical separation may reveal a conscious desire on the part of both groups to essentially maintain the integrity of their own cultural systems.[53] It is also speculated that they may have desired separate settlements because "the Black Seminoles were emerging as a distinct people at this time and . . . were developing their own unique culture."[54]

Intermarriages between Seminoles and Black Seminoles did occur, though not extensively. Upon marriage to Seminole Indian women, Black Seminoles "became Indians or free citizens, [enjoying] equal privileges with them."[55] Black Seminoles maintained the tradition of patrilineal descent (as differentiated from Seminole matrilineal descent), as well as African naming practices that conferred upon a newborn the name for that day of the week or month of the year. In fact, two men named July and August were community leaders and valued interpreters for the Seminoles.[56]

The Seminoles' knowledge of agriculture, owing to their Creek ancestry, included the cultivation of maize (corn), beans, and a variety of vegetables. The Africans, many of whom originated from the rice-growing regions of West Africa, shared their expertise in rice cultivation and other agricultural techniques.[57]

Persistent forays into Florida by militias, including those from Georgia and Tennessee, destroyed Seminole and Black Seminole settlements, forcing their relocation to other areas of the state where they could enjoy increased security. They sought refuge in less accessible areas, such as swamps and hammocks. The siting of these refuges resembled the pattern of traditional maroon communities that were always located in the most formidable environments available.

"Black towns" associated with the Seminole towns in Florida can be understood both as maroon communities—whose members were constantly prepared for guerrilla warfare[58]—and as structural components of the Seminole town. United States Army major George McCall recorded the following account (1826) of a visit to the Black Seminole town of Peliklakaha (also known as Abraham's Old Town), situated twelve miles south of Okahumpka, where Micanopy established a Seminole town after the 1813 destruction of his Alachua settlements:

On the third day we reached "*Pelahlikaha*"—in English, "Many Ponds." In the midst of these ponds, on a ridge of high "shell-hummock" land . . . there now flourishes one of the most prosperous Negro towns in the Indian territory. We found the Negroes in possession of large fields of the finest land, producing large crops of corn, beans, melons, pumpkins and other esculent vegetables. They are chiefly runaway slaves from Georgia, who have put themselves under the protection of Micanopy...to whom, for this consideration, they render a tribute of one-third of the produce of the land, and one-third of the horses, cattle and fowls they may raise. Otherwise they are free to come and go at pleasure, and in some cases are elevated to the position of equality with their masters. I saw while riding along the borders of the ponds fine rice growing; and in the village large corn-cribs well filled, while the houses were larger and more comfortable than those of the Indians themselves. The three principal men bear the distinguished names of July, August and Abram. We found these men to be shrewd, intelligent fellows, and to the highest degree of obsequious.[59]

An archaeological survey of the site of Peliklakaha in Sumter County yielded materials indicating that the site was occupied from 1813 to 1836, and that it was almost certainly a Black Seminole site.[60] Recent excavations at the site have recovered many artifacts that

offer the most tangible evidence of the ancient inhabitants' activities and belongings. Pipe stem fragments [that] were once a part of long clay pipes smoked by townspeople.... "[B]rushed" pots whose fragments now lay scattered about the site . . . [were used] to prepare *Soffkee,* a dish resembling pudding that was made from the coontie plant root. Crumbling, rusty fragments are all that remain of metal tools and kettles used at Abraham's Old Town. A 19th century soldier reported seeing ball-sticks, Indian flutes, and tortoise shell rattles in the charred ruins of Abraham's town. These instruments were used in communal ceremonies. Pieces of European ironstone china platters, pearlware plates, and stoneware mugs and crocks are the most numerous type of artifact left at the site. These goods were obtained from trading and raiding expeditions to plantations and colonial settlements.... They adorned themselves in fancy white-metal conical earrings.... We have found blue, green, and clear glass beads in a few excavation units.[61]

The population of Peliklakaha in 1823 is estimated at 160 persons, and the town's principal men were July, August, and Abraham, who served as interpreters. Peliklakaha was reputed to be "one of the most prosperous Negro towns in Indian Territory...in possession of large fields of the finest land, [and] producing large crops."[62] The town was ultimately destroyed by fire. Some other Black Seminole settlements were King Heijah's Town, located in Alachua County;

Negro Town, located near the Withlacoochee River; Boggy (Kettle) Island, associated with the Alachua Seminoles; Sitarkey, located between Camp Izard and Fort King in west Florida. Still other "Negro Towns" were located in the vicinity of Bowleg's Town along the Suwannee River.[63]

In addition to their mutual cause of halting Euroamerican expansion into Florida, another bond between the Africans and the Seminoles, I suggest, was spiritual. Despite their inter- and intragroup cultural diversity, many African and indigenous peoples shared an underlying worldview. Worldviews are rarely explicitly stated, yet strongly influence behavior. This worldview included belief in the following: a Supreme Creator who is unknowable and sacred, contact with whom requires the intercession of lesser beings, specifically, "spirit helpers" (indigenous) and "orishas" (African, Yoruba nation); a spirit world that exists side by side with, and intermingles with, the physical world; the interrelatedness and dynamic interdependence of all life forms; the harmony ethos; wellness as harmony in spirit, mind, and body, generated from within rather than from without; the circle, symbolic of immortality and existence that is circular versus linear; art and religion as integral parts of everyday life, not objectified; an oral tradition; and the mystical power of women. Coincidence of worldview between peoples can have extensive ramifications; in the case of Seminoles and Black Seminoles, it apparently led to a situation of cultural compatibility that likely strengthened their relationship. The Creeks and Seminoles have always been highly secretive about their sacred Green Corn Dance ritual, therefore no direct evidence exists about the exact practices or participants.[64] Yet because of the close relationship between the two groups, it is possible that some Black Seminoles may have been invited to take part in this sacred ceremony.

Black Seminoles became increasingly indispensable to the Seminoles. Many were multilingual, fluent in indigenous languages, including the Seminoles' Muskogean dialect, as well as English, Spanish, and French. These linguistic skills facilitated interaction with Euroamericans on behalf of the Seminoles in treaty negotiations. According to Georgia runaway-advertisements from 1763 to 1790, the vast majority had good to very good levels of English proficiency, as well as proficiency in other African and European languages.[65]

Ironically, Black Seminoles also negotiated slave ownership disputes between Seminoles and Euroamericans. Two of the most prominent black interpreters were Abraham and Cudjo. Abraham is described as "plausible, pliant and deceitful," having a great deal of influence over the Indian nation. "With an appearance of great modesty, he is ambitious, avaricious and, withal very intelligent."[66] In his capacity of interpreter, Abraham accompanied a Seminole delegation to Washington. Cudjo, on the other hand, was a regular interpreter at the Seminole agency. He sided with the government at Removal time, possibly because he was partially paralyzed and needed medical attention that was available only from Euroamerican doctors.[67]

The Black Seminoles also spoke an "Afro-Seminole" creole language that combined West African grammar with English lexicon and resembles the Gullah language of the Sea Islanders of South Carolina and Georgia.[68] Rebecca Bateman, an anthropologist who conducted research among the Black Seminoles in Oklahoma, states that

> the blacks who became associated with the Seminole in Florida most likely ... spoke an English-based creole language. We know that this last point is plausible because linguist Ian Hancock (1975, 1977, 1980) discovered that older Seminoles of Brackettville, Texas, had retained knowledge of an English-based creole, which Hancock termed "Afro-Seminole Creole" that was very similar to Gullah. The evidence indicates that this creole was also spoken in the Oklahoma and Mexico communities [where Black Seminoles migrated], and probably the Andros Black Seminole settlement as well. The blacks spoke Creek/Seminole with the Indians, but probably the creole within their own communities. Thus, the Black Seminole, while they did adopt some Seminole cultural practices, retained a significant degree of cultural, linguistic, and political autonomy throughout their history.[69]

The Seminole Wars

Ultimately, Euroamericans' fears of alliances between indigenous peoples and Africans materialized when the Seminoles and Black Seminoles joined forces against them in the Patriots War of 1812.[70] The Seminoles initially planned to remain neutral in what they believed was a "fight between white men," but in response to Seminole chief King Payne's request,[71] and Spanish governor Kindelan's persuasion, they elected to join the battle against the Euroamericans. This encounter marked the beginning of over forty years of warfare in the southeastern United States.

Negro Fort

A major event in this ongoing warfare occurred in 1816 along the Apalachicola River in Florida. The British erected Fort Blount, more commonly known as Negro Fort, during their occupation of Florida from 1763 to 1783. When the British were forced to relinquish control of Florida to the Spanish in 1783,[72] the fort's command was assumed by Black Seminole officers; three hundred Seminole and Black Seminole men, women, and children were resident there.[73] Negro Fort was a haven for runaways, who eventually settled inside of or adjacent to the protective fort, establishing farms for fifty miles along the Apalachicola River. Free Africans living so near the borders of slave states outraged Euroamericans, and in July 1816 the United States Navy launched an attack on the fort. It was destroyed when one cannonball fortuitously struck its gunpowder magazine. Most of the estimated fifty survivors were returned to enslavement in Georgia. Others died from their injuries. A few escaped and joined Chief Billy Bowlegs's villages along the Suwannee River.[74]

The First Seminole War: 1817–1818

General Andrew Jackson's troops and their Creek allies marched on Florida, destroying Miccosukee and Suwannee River settlements that were home to both Seminoles and Black Seminoles. His troops, initially unsuccessful at rooting out the African and Seminole insurgents—who took refuge in the swamps after inflicting a decisive blow to Jackson's forces—claimed a victorious end to a battle that ultimately was won by destroying villages occupied by women and children.[75]

The invasion was motivated by the desire to acquire land and, more importantly, to eliminate the safe haven that Florida afforded runaways from Georgia and South Carolina. Their buffer zone destroyed, and their troops severely outnumbered, the Spanish conceded the Florida territory to the United States in the 1819 Adams-Onís Treaty.[76] The Spanish departed for Cuba, taking along with them 145 free Africans.[77] Although the $5 million paid to the Spanish for the Florida territory was represented as a real estate purchase, Jackson's incursion can more accurately be defined as a blatant seizure of sovereign Spanish territory.

After Florida was ceded to the United States, the government drafted treaties that assigned plots of land to free Africans who remained in Florida. Consistent with virtually all treaties that the United States government ever signed with North American indigenous peoples, the agreements made with these free Africans were not honored. Euroamericans who migrated to Florida found the prospect of coexisting with free, property-owning Africans intolerable and forced them to sell their lands. Landless and no longer under the protection of the Spanish, some Africans elected to join the Spaniards' exodus to Cuba.[78] Others chose to enlist with the Seminoles and continue the fight against Euroamerican aggressors, whose focus was trained even more intently on removing all of the Seminoles from valuable land in Florida and reenslaving the Black Seminoles.

The Treaty of Moultrie Creek

In 1823, an agreement was signed at Moultrie Creek (located south of St. Augustine) that negotiated a cession of lands occupied by Seminoles and Black Seminoles in northern Florida in exchange for a southern tract of reportedly 5 million acres. This cession included the fertile Alachua lands "where the descendants of Cowkeeper, founder of the Seminole nation, had lived for more than two generations."[79] The treaty promised that they would be paid approximately $13,000 to compensate them for relocation expenses, given subsistence provisions (for one year), a school, and a blacksmith.[80] The agreement also required the Seminoles to be "active and vigilant in preventing the retreating to, or passing through, of the district assigned to them, of any absconding slaves, or fugitives from justice and to deliver all such people to the agent and be compensated for their expenses."[81] This treaty proved disastrous for the Seminoles. The promised rations were inadequate, and the land assigned to them was not fit for cultivation.

Removal

The Indian Removal Act, signed by President Jackson on May 28, 1830, stipulated that the Seminoles and most other indigenous nations in the southeastern United States (including the Cherokees, Choctaws, Chickasaws, Creeks) must relocate to Indian Territory, an area west of the Mississippi River in present-day Oklahoma and Kansas. The Indian Removal was an attempt to resolve the "Indian problem" for Americans who wanted to settle on indigenous peoples' lands, but in Florida it was just as much an attempt to finally solve the "Negro Problem."[82] Notably Micanopy, Coa Hadjo, Jumper, and Osceola resisted relocation to Indian Territory. Another influential person opposing relocation was Abraham, Micanopy's chief interpreter, who along with John Caesar, another prominent Black Seminole leader, actively worked to prevent the Removal.[83] The influence of Osceola in many events during this period has often been exaggerated. Although he did wield influence among the Seminoles, he was actually a lower-level leader, a war chief. Osceola adamantly opposed reunification with the Creeks, who had already been removed to Indian Territory, and who had long since become the Seminoles' sworn enemies. Osceola's rage against Euroamericans reached a climax when his wife—denigrated by the U.S. government's Seminole agent, General Wiley Thompson, as merely a "halfbreed" Black Seminole—was captured by a slave-catcher and subsequently died, possibly of her own hand, after killing her captor.[84]

Designed as yet another attempt to persuade recalcitrant Seminoles to agree to move to Indian Territory, the 1832 Treaty of Payne's Landing provided for a delegation of seven Seminole chiefs—selected by Euroamericans—to inspect Creek lands west of the Mississippi. If they found the land favorable and the Creeks were willing to reunite with them as one tribe, an agreement to remove to Indian Territory within three years would be binding. On March 28, 1833, at Fort Gibson in Indian Territory, the Seminole delegation signed a second treaty on behalf of all Seminoles, although they had not been granted such authority from other Seminole leaders. A stumbling block in the negotiations was the disposition of the Black Seminoles living among them. The Seminoles feared that if their Black Seminole allies (and some were probably family members) accompanied them to Indian Territory, Creeks loyal to the Euroamericans would try to seize and reenslave them. The Seminoles were acutely aware that Creeks, like Cherokees, practiced a harsher system of slavery than did the Seminoles. Black Seminole interpreters continued to use their considerable influence to persuade the Seminoles not to leave Florida, fearing negative consequences for themselves. Euroamericans in Florida also attempted to dissuade the Seminoles from taking their "property" to Indian Territory, but not out of concern for the Black Seminoles' security. This tactic was a surreptitious plot to seize Black Seminoles *legally*, as soon as the fugitive slave laws of the United States were extended to Florida. Black Seminoles' worst fears were realized when they eventually moved to Indian Territory. After the Seminoles signed a treaty with the Creeks in Indian Territory in January 1845, ending their long-standing hostilities, Seminole–Black Seminole relations rapidly deteriorated. The Fugitive Slave Law of 1850 permitted entry into Indian Territory for recovery of lost "property" or persons who ostensibly owed former "masters" their services.

The Second Seminole War: 1835–1842

The bloody and protracted Second Seminole War commenced on December 28, 1835. Several key incidents sparked it: the capture and imprisonment of Osceola in an attempt to force him to agree to the Treaty of Payne's Landing;[85] singling out Black Seminole leaders as targets for assassination in order to eliminate their influence over the Seminoles; and plantation raids by King Phillip's Seminole and Black Seminole forces. Despite treaty promises to preserve Seminole rights, Euroamericans "thought they had a doubtless right to do with the Indian, or his property, as they might think proper. . . . but as the Indian's evidence could not be received in a court of justice, the white man's oath would condemn him to the most torturing punishment."[86] Persistent depredations on their rights and property prompted the leaders of ten Seminole towns to send a letter to the commander at Fort Hawkins, likely inscribed by one of the Black Seminole interpreters, complaining that, "[t]here is nothing said about what white people do—but all that the Indians do is brought up. The cattle that we are accused of taking, were cattle that the white people took from us—our young men went out and brought them back with the same marks and brands."[87]

Frustrated by broken treaty conditions and the lack of judicial redress, the Seminoles' only resort was war, the Second Seminole War. Attacks by Osceola's warriors and those of Micanopy, Alligator, and Jumper, which included contingents of Black Seminoles, resulted in the deaths of Indian agent Thompson at Fort King and troops commanded by Major Francis L. Dade.[88] The Second Seminole War was to prove the costliest ever fought in the United States in terms of human and financial resources. The ranks of the Seminole–Black Seminole alliance were constantly replenished with Africans who escaped Florida plantations; "With the friendliness of the Seminole Indians, the relative inexperience of Florida slaveowners in methods and practices of slavery, and a number of other reasons, the number of Negroes who escaped or attempted escape was still high in the state by about 1835–40."[89]

General Thomas Sidney Jesup, commander of United States troops, recognized that the "defeat of the Seminoles depended on the defeat or surrender of the blacks, who represented some of their fiercest and most intelligent warriors and leaders."[90] Beginning around 1836, he separated the majority of Black Seminoles from the Seminole Indians. Jesup classified blacks into the following categories: (1) those captured by a regiment of Creek warriors who were under contract to fight the Seminoles; (2) those protected by the convention of Fort Dade, March 6, 1837; (3) those captured by United States troops, including those who separated voluntarily from their Indian masters and came in; (4) those who came in with Alligator and his band in April 1838; (5) those brought in by their owners and sent west with them; and (6) those really the property of white men but not claimed by or returned to their owners before emigration. This taxonomy did not satisfy some Euroamericans. Because of disputed "claims" made by a few families (e.g., Humphreys, Creeks, Love, Watson, and Forrester) for ownership of the blacks, another outbreak of war threatened to erupt before the Removal. General Jesup was anxious to conclude the removal process and, consequently, reclassified blacks into four categories: (1) descendants of blacks taken from the first citizens of Georgia by the Creek Confederacy in former wars, for which the citizens had been indemnified; (2) blacks purchased by the Indians from Spanish authorities and from other individuals; (3) blacks taken from plantations before the Treaty of Payne's Landing; and (4) blacks claimed under pretended purchases from the Indians.[91]

The Seminoles, starving and landless, finally surrendered and resolved to migrate to Indian Territory. Approximately 240 Black Seminoles migrated to Indian Territory with them. They left in several groups, over a period of about one year, from Tampa Bay.[92] Some of the Black Seminoles who had lived among them for many years were left behind, either imprisoned or returned to slaveowners who anxiously swept into Florida to claim their property before the impending removal west. Others escaped, withdrew further into the swamps, and lived to fight yet another war with the Americans.

The Third Seminole War: 1855

A congressional act declared that all indigenous peoples were banned from Florida; this precipitated the third and final Seminole War. A definitive victory for the United States in this war was elusive; approximately two hundred Seminoles and Black Seminoles escaped into the Big Cypress Swamp and the Everglades, which ultimately proved to be impenetrable by the United States troops. The swamps were formidable but were familiar territory to the Seminoles and Black Seminoles, who lured the Americans into traps where they would be severely cut by the sharp sawgrass prevalent there. Ultimately, the Euroamericans abandoned their pursuit.

These surviving maroons were the genesis of today's Seminole Indians in Florida. Following is an anonymously written story from the *Miami Daily News* about the death of Jimmie Osceola, a Seminole whose family was among the few to successfully resist removal and remain in Florida. I cite it in its entirety because it illustrates so well the history and heartbreak of those who remained. Jimmie Osceola committed suicide.

JIMMIE OSCEOLA, 95, DIES IN BIG CYPRESS;
FOUGHT U[.]S[.] IN SEMINOLES' LAST STAND

Sept. 9, 1946

Jimmie Osceola, who fought under Billy Bowlegs when the Seminoles made their last stand 70 years ago against US troops in what is now Collier County, died yesterday in the Big Cypress. He was 95 and, according to Indian Agent Kenneth Marmon, probably the oldest living Seminole. In the veins of Jimmie Osceola ran the blood of his ancestor, the great Chief Osceola. Proud and taciturn to the last, he lived in one of the last wilderness areas of the nation, the Big Cypress. It was into this stronghold that the Seminoles were forced by the steady encroachments of the whites during the last century. Here Billy Bowlegs, for whom Billy's creek in Fort Myers was named, rallied the remaining young men of the bands, carefully hid the women and children in the swamps, and made his last effort to turn back the white man. The bloody campaign that followed found federal troops based at the military post known as Ft. Myers. After months of guerrilla warfare, Billy Bowlegs agreed to an armistice and many of the half-starved Seminoles came into the fort for removal to Oklahoma. Jimmie Osceola refused to surrender to the whites and, although he put down his arms, there was evidence that he never forgave the invader for broken treaties and treachery. Billy Bowlegs was the last chief of the Seminoles. Jimmie Osceola might well have succeeded to that position, but in the bitterness of defeat, the Seminoles, who respected as many treaties as the whites broke, agreed to a condition that the "dangerous" office be kept vacant. Little is known of the Seminole side of the three wars in which they defied the white man's aggression. Jimmie Osceola, perhaps the last living link with that era, carried his secrets with him.

Today, approximately 2,000 Seminole Indians reside on Florida reservations in Hollywood, Big Cypress, Brighton, Immokalee, and Tampa. Others live in adjacent cities and often commute to and from the reservations. The majority of them are organized as the Seminole Tribe of Florida, which was incorporated in 1957. The Miccosukee Indians split from the Seminoles that year and established separate reservations in south Florida. Both proudly claim the distinction of being the only "unconquered" indigenous peoples of North America.

3 ⊚⊚

The Promised Island

Andros, Bahamas

At the end of the First Seminole War, the United States annexed the former Spanish territory of Florida and Euroamericans migrated there in accelerated fashion. Their persistent encroachment upon former indigenous lands forced the Seminole Indians and Black Seminoles living there to retreat into marronage, taking refuge in the swamps and hammocks of southern Florida. They were being "driven from their homes and hunted as wild deer."[1] While the primary concern for the Seminoles was banishment from their homes and removal to Indian Territory in the West, the Black Seminoles feared recapture, which meant either return to enslavement or summary death.[2]

Broken Promises

The Seminoles perceived the Bahamas as "a natural refuge for Seminole Negroes"[3] and themselves because of alliances forged with the British in Florida and long-standing trade relations established with them in the Bahamas. The cordiality of Native American–Bahamian relations was demonstrated in the March 1, 1817, issue of the *Bahamas Royal Gazette,* which announced "Heeleisaja a chief of the Creek Nation of Indians and his son sailed on the Blucher for London."

The British had promised to reward the Seminoles with military and economic support in return for their loyalty during the siege of New Orleans. Accordingly, the Florida Seminole leaders, desperate for assistance in their struggle against the Euroamericans, sought to take advantage of the British offer. A consensus was reached that Chief Kenadgie, a tribal elder, should travel "to New Providence [Bahamas] or Jamaica for the purpose of stating their grievances and soliciting assistance" from the British.[4] Chief Kenadgie arrived at New Providence Island, Bahamas, via dugout canoe on September 29, 1819, accompanied by several others, including an interpreter described as "an Indian of mixed blood." The interpreter may have been Abraham, a Black Seminole who often negotiated on behalf of the Seminoles with the Euroamericans as Chief Micanopy's personal interpreter. They complained to the British that their people in Florida were being persistently tormented, and that "their greatest enemies [were] the Cowetas . . . who having made terms with the Americans [were] set on them to harass and annihilate their tribe."[5] When Chief Kenadgie appealed to the British for aid, however, the British reneged on their promises to buttress the Seminoles' cause. British officials in Nassau, New Providence, advised that because of the recent peace treaty signed with the United States of America, the British nation was not inclined to interfere in the Seminoles' current dispute.[6] Kenadgie and his fellow travelers were provided with food and shelter on New Providence for one week, and summarily returned to Florida via the British schooner *Primrose* with their canoe in tow.[7]

Another party of Seminole Indians arrived on New Providence two years later. This time, however, the Seminoles had no express motive for their visit.[8] Ten of them had arrived destitute and in need of food and clothing. In a futile gesture of loyalty, one member of their party proudly displayed his Certificate of Gallantry and Good Conduct, awarded for service with the British troops in Florida during the War of 1812.[9] Once again, the British leaders offered only provisions to the Seminoles, and then sent them back to Florida.

Several months after the second group of Seminole Indians returned to Florida in 1821, a third group made plans to depart for the Bahamas. This group was much larger and probably consisted mostly of Black Seminoles.[10] After years of struggle to survive the increasingly hostile situation in Florida, they fled to the Bahamas, where they hoped to live as free men and women. They secretly congregated at Cape Florida and embarked in whatever transport they could secure, whether dugout canoes or wreckers. Wreckers were ships that were employed in searching for and salvaging wrecked cargo vessels—a lucrative business along the Florida coast at that time. Cargo ships, lacking lighthouse beacons to guide them at night, would crash upon the reefs, spilling their cargoes. These cargoes were salvaged by the wrecker captains and crews and sold to Nassau customers. James Mott, a privateer, commanded one of these ships, the *Sheerwater*, and he reportedly facilitated the escape of a large group of Black Seminoles.[11] Harry A. Kersey, Jr., an ethnohistorian, speculates that most of the journeys that brought this third group of Seminoles to the Bahamas occurred between 1821 and 1837, and that "it is not known just how many perished or survived in this exodus . . . but it was an epic journey born of desperation which has a modern counterpart in the Haitian and Cuban 'boat people.'"[12]

The Seminoles' previous trips to the Bahamas had clearly demonstrated the futility of their efforts to secure aid from the British on New Providence, so they altered their strategy. This time they chose to land not on New Providence, but on the western shore of Andros Island, a large Out Island of the Bahamas approximately 25 miles west of New Providence and 150 miles from the Florida coast. A few landed in the Biminis and on Joulter Cay; many of these later joined the majority of the Black Seminole and Seminole refugees, who had settled at Red Bays, Andros Island.

Andros Island

Early navigational charts indicate that Andros Island was originally named La Isla del Espiritu Santo by the Spaniards. However, the origin of its current designation has been variously described. It may have been named for Sir Edmund Andros, British commander of the forces in Barbados in 1672 and colonial governor in America from 1674 to 1689, although there is no evidence that he ever set foot on the island. In 1787 the island became the sanctuary for approximately 1,400 Loyalist refugees from the island of San Andrés off the Mosquito Coast of Nicaragua when Spain took possession of it under the 1783 Treaty of Paris between Spain and Britain—the refugees may have transferred the name of their former home to their new one. It may also be that the island was named after the Greek island of St. Andro: Greek merchants on the island exported sponges harvested from the bountiful sponge beds of the mud flats around Andros Island for almost one hundred years.[13]

The settlement of Red Bays, where the critical mass of Black Seminole descendants reside, is located on the northwestern tip of Andros, one of the Family Islands of the Bahamas. The Family Islands were formerly known as the "Out Islands"; the name was changed after Bahamians gained their independence in 1973, and it refers to all islands other than New Providence, site of the capital city, Nassau.

The largest island in the Bahamian archipelago—104 miles in length and 40 miles wide—Andros has three sociopolitical divisions, separated by naturally occurring bights and mangrove-bordered creeks. These divisions are North Andros, Central Andros, and South Andros.[14] The Grand Bahama Bank borders the island's western side, while the Tongue of the Ocean, one thousand fathoms deep, borders the eastern coast. A line of reefs runs along the east coast and forms a natural harbor bordering one of the largest reefs in the world, after that in Australia. Andros is also the fifth largest island in the circum-Caribbean region, following Cuba, Hispaniola, Jamaica, and Puerto Rico.

Today, the population of Andros includes a small number of white Bahamians and immigrants from various other countries, but approximately 95 percent of the 8,000 Androsians are of predominantly or entirely African descent and are locally known as black Bahamians. Andros Island has the reputation of being the richest repository of African culture in the Bahamas, as demonstrated in its social and economic structures and religious traditions.[15]

The Function of Oral Tradition

The primary objective of my research on Andros Island was to record and analyze the oral history of Black Seminole descendants there. One of the major catalysts for this research was the publications of anthropologist John Goggin, who worked there in the 1930s and 1940s. Felix MacNeil's personal narrative, recorded by Goggin in 1937, correlates with the oral tradition of Andros residents whom I interviewed more than fifty years later, in 1996 and 1997. Oral traditions are "messages transmitted beyond the generation that gave rise to them," and like personal narratives, they can function as a means to validate one's life by "making sense of various experiences lived through and, in a sense, created through the narrative."[16] More than mere testimonies to the past, oral traditions are "of interest as structured aesthetic and personal creations in the present."[17] Because most if not all of the Black Seminole immigrants were illiterate, the best means of maintaining their family histories was by means of oral tradition. Black Seminoles' understanding of the past, and their relationship to it, is contextualized in this social memory—the unwritten collective oral accounts passed down through generations.[18]

The oral tradition of the Black Seminoles in the Bahamas—as related to me by Red Bays residents in my interviews, and published by the Reverend Bertram A. Newton in his pamphlet *A History of Red Bays, Andros, Bahamas*—broadly conforms to an "account," something that Jan Vansina defines as a story "fused out of several accounts [that] has acquired a stabilized form,"[19] and whose content has a precise, yet unobservable, function in society. These functions become clear when a causal relationship can be demonstrated, that is, when it can be demonstrated to have benefit to party X or party Y. The detection of the relationship, then, allows us to uncover its purpose. An accurate perspective of the purpose or function that a particular oral tradition performs in a society requires sociohistorical knowledge of a community, a context within which to make an interpretation. As such, a diachronic analysis of the publication of Bertram Newton's *History* reveals that its 1968 release occurred in a critical context of sociopolitical change in Red Bays and the Bahamas in general: 1968 was the year that a logging company cleared a road through the dense pineyard into Red Bays, permitting unprecedented access into, and out of, Red Bays and as a result, tremendous new opportunities for commerce and education for its residents; in 1967 the country elected its first black Bahamian prime minister, Sir Lynden Pindling.

Oral Tradition of Bahamian Black Seminoles

Following are excerpts from interviews that I recorded with Andros Island consultants who traced their Seminole Indian heritage. The majority of the narratives included here are from residents of the settlement of Red Bays. Two of the interviews, however, are with persons whose ancestors settled in other areas of Andros Island. The oral tradition is relatively consistent and emphasizes the fundamental courage and tenacity of those Black Seminoles whose journey originated long ago on the plantations of Georgia, South Carolina, and Florida. Their recreation of identity and culture in the Bahamas was grounded in the synthesis of heritage and adaptation.

The Reverend Bertram A. Newton—Red Bays

Bertram A. Newton has lived in Red Bays for all but one of his seventy-one years. The one year he was away from home he was attending Teachers College in Nassau. He returned to become principal of Red Bays All-Age School (later named Red Bays Primary School). Newton credits Pastor Joseph Lewis, whose grandfather Sammy Lewis was an original Red Bays settler, as the source of most of the information contained in the *History*.[20] Newton is a community leader: in addition to being the former principal and teacher of the school, he is the pastor of the settlement's only church—New Salem Baptist. Newton views the project of recording the oral tradition of Red Bays as an imperative for posterity. As he says, "[It] is going to be very, very important for the oncoming generation, say, like my grandchildren and like the great-grand that will come after."[21]

He traces matrilineal and patrilineal descent from the original settlers. His great-grandfather, Moses Newton, was named on the 1828 customs roster which listed the names of persons seized and taken to Nassau by the customs agent (see fig. 3). Bertram Newton is "the son of Rev. Eldrack Eneas Newton and Adranna Newton Dean. Adranna was born at Red Bays Andros to Ellen Dean Pinder and Eldrack Newton was born in Staniard Creek Andros, that's Central Andros. He was the son of Arthur Newton, [who was] the son of Moses Newton, one of the Seminole Indians who came from Florida about 1845."

Eldrack Newton "was born in 1900 and went to the [world] war in 1914. After he came from the war, he had nothing to do. He came down sponging at Red Bays, saw Adranna, marry her, settle here. Adranna was the granddaughter of Mary Lewis, also a Seminole Indian that came from Florida with her brothers and those, Watkin Lewis and her father Sammy Lewis. They have had together, well my mother told me eighteen children and I was about the second. But only nine were known to live."

RH: Can you tell me whether they [the original settlers] were full-blood Indian, or were they mixed Indian and African?

BN: Mixed. Yes mixed. But Moses Newton and Sammy Lewis they had full resemblance of Indians and I have not gotten the history whether they were full-blooded or not. But it is my opinion that they were because of the description of their faces. And so, Eldrack Newton came here sponging on the boat because in those days, sponge was the main industry here in the Bahamas. And ... as many as one hundred and thirty-eight, or something like that, boats would come out here from all throughout the Bahamas and come down to Red Bays sponging, which they call mud sponging because the sponge was gotten on the Mud. They would rest on corals and then you find them in the mud holes. They would surge themselves until they get in holes. Even now today people go out here and sponge.

There was a settlement of those persons who never stopped at Red Bays or congregated at Red Bays: Nicholls Town, Lowe Sound, and the Joulter Cays. They went right straight on up the shore and they stopped in Staniard Creek. There may not be any now alive, but I sure that there are descendants like the Bowlegs, Russells, the MacNeils, and the Demerittes.

There was a medicine doctor came along with them. He was good on bush medicine. Once someone in the group get sick, he would go in the bush and find the medicine. He was called Scipio Demeritte [actually Bowleg].

RH: Did he pass his trade along to his family members?

BN: Well I believe so because my mother-in-law, Omelia Marshall, is now known to be called the bush doctor here in Red Bays. When people got sick, she would go in the bush and can recommend different medicine to people. She is the granddaughter [of Scipio Bowleg, the bush doctor whom MacNeil told Goggin about].

Benjamin Lewis—Red Bays

The Reverend Benjamin Lewis is a sixty-nine-year-old retired seaman and construction worker who now serves as the associate pastor of Red Bays' New Salem Baptist Church. He was off island working in Nassau as a carpenter for twenty years. It was during this time that his father, Joseph Lewis, related the history of Red Bays to Bertram Newton. Benjamin Lewis returned home after his father got sick and remained in Red Bays after his father's death at age eighty-four. Benjamin Lewis remembered:

He [Joseph Lewis] let me know that I'm a part of the Seminole Indians. My great-grandfather was Sammy Lewis, which was his grandfather. He came from Florida in a canoe and the first place they rested was at Cedar Coppitt. Later on down, they move from Cedar Coppitt and they went up into a lake and they came into a little island and he fall in love with the little island, and he give it name Sammy Lewis after him.

He stood there for while, and after, he thought it is fit that he travel someplace else. He start traveling down north till he reach a place down here which he call Red Bay. And he was there until an hurricane came, and this hurricane overflow the place. And they leave from there and they came up here to the place call Lewis Coppitt. This place was a huge coppitt, and one day my grandfather, Watkin Lewis, this was Sammy Lewis' son, he went through this coppitt and he began to search through it and went to come back out, he got lost and been in there almost a whole day. They used to call it "Lost Man Coppitt." After which he purchased sixty-one-and-three-quarter-acre ground and give it name Lewis Coppitt. And the Lewises were the first to settle here in this little part of Andros which is the last tip of North Andros call Red Bay.

But this place is formerly known as Lewis Coppitt. And he preside here and he raise up his sons and daughters and after departure of the old man Sammy Lewis, then Watkin Lewis and his children stood here. And later on there are some others come in and join with them and make this to become a settlement. The majority of the people living here are mostly branch off from the Seminole descendant [sic]. Because he had daughters and sons and they marry, and they children grew and the others come in and marry to they children, and they grandchildren. And therefore, this settlement become an outstanding settlement as it is today. We the people of Red Bay we give God the glory for the old patriarch Sammy Lewis who had made preparation for this coming generation. And that is why we, the Lewises people, is call the Seminole descent. There were the MacNeils and the Bowlegs what join along with those people.

Today we have lots of different descendants. We have the Russells, we have the Colebrookes, we have the Marshalls, we have the Newtons, we have the Barrs, we have the Taylors, we have the Knowles, we have the Motts, and many others who came in and made this little township a success.[22]

William Colebrooke—Red Bays

"Old Iron," or "Scrap Iron," as William Colebrooke is known to most local people, tells me that he is sixty-one years of age. He earned his livelihood on the sea until someone stole his boat. He still occasionally goes out to sea, fishing with other men from the settlement, and makes crabbing trips in season. As a rule he is a solitary character. Old Iron now makes his living sewing baskets.[23] He is noted for sewing some of the largest baskets ever crafted in Red Bays, including the one he made for me that measures 34 inches in height and 160 inches in circumference. He often served as my guide; we biked three miles through the bush, mostly along an overgrown former logging road, to the site of the original Red Bays settlement. Old Iron related to me:

> In the years past, when the war was on, the people, the Seminolians from Florida, travel by canoes from Florida and the first place they end up was Big Cross Cay, then come into Red Bay. And from Red Bay they settle there for a while. Some of them stop at Red Bay and some of them travel on from Cedar Coppitt to go down the shore as far as come round up to Driggs Hill, Behring Point, come round Mangrove Cay, Long Bay Cay, and all of them, and come straight up round there to on the east side of Andros. Maybe some may gone into Nassau, I don't know.

RH: Were your great-grandparents some of the original settlers?

WC: Um-hum, such as Mary Russell, Pa Watkin, and amongst them. And John Lewis, Shaddy Lewis, and so on. When a hurricane come down the place flood and they move from there [original Red Bays site] and come up to Red Bay . . . this place now. At first they call it Lewis Coppitt because one set of the Lewis was here first, and the other set was down to Red Bay. Then the main boss who was over all of them come up here, then all decide to live at Lewis Coppitt. Then after all the old folks dead out, then [Rev.] B. A. Newton say we'll change the name from Lewis Coppitt to Red Bay. That's how this place get to call Red Bay. This place is not [the original] Red Bay. This happen in the early part. What time I can't remember. My great-grandma, Ma Mary, all of them come from Florida.[24]

Frederick Russell—Red Bays

The Reverend Frederick Russell, sixty-eight years old at the time I interviewed him in 1996, died in 1999. He was born and raised in Red Bays. For many years he served as a deacon in Red Bays' New Salem Baptist Church, and at the time of his death he was the pastor of Mizpah Baptist Church in Nicholls Town. Russell was one of only a few older-generation Red Bays residents who received any formal education beyond primary school. By his own admission, Russell may not have known the history as well as Bertram Newton:

> I spend a majority of my life off from here, in Nassau. I was a train nurse at the Princess Margaret Hospital. I grew up here, I had my education here in the All-Age School, called E. E. Newton All-Age School. The highest grade was then grade four and I went through grade four. After I left school I went to Nassau. I was then nineteen years old. My father name was Joshua Shadrack Russell and my mother name was Leanora Russell and they both are dead now. They were very poor people. They was a part of the Seminole Indians descendant. My father, his mother was a sister of the Lewis, Sam Lewis, who was an Indian. He came here from Florida I heard, and my daddy was one of her sons. He got married to my mother, Leanora Newton from Staniard Creek.
>
> My father['s] mother was Celeste Russell. I can't remember her. When she died I was very small then. Her father was Watkin Lewis, and it was couple a those brothers, it was Sam those men, I heard, came from there [Florida] in a boat, in a canoe. My mother['s] father, or my grandfather, was also an Indian [Moses Newton, his name listed in fig. 3]. Now all of those men did not stay in one community. They separated. My mother['s] father went into Staniard Creek, that's in Central Andros. That's where my mother was born. And Watkin Lewis, he stop here. They travel from Cedar Coppitt area, that's about ten miles, or maybe more, from here where we are. And they travel along the shore until they get here. I heard that one of those Indians went into Conch Sound.
>
> They [the Lewises] had Indian blood and one stop into Mastic Point I think, and so on, but they separate themselves from each others, and then they married, they get children, and all of they children become their generation, and so we call the whole body of Indians, the Seminole Indians, a generation.[25]

Alma (Prudence) Miller—Lowe Sound

I found Alma Miller, at sixty-nine years young tending her small garden when I approached her house. Skillfully wielding a cutlass,[26] she chopped the weeds away from her small crop of cassava, eddy (local name for the edible root of the eddo plant, commonly found in the tropics), and corn in the yard next to her house. She welcomed me into her home, eager to share with me what she remembers about her Seminole Indian heritage. She is a tall, "bright," striking woman; it is easy to understand why, in younger years, she bore the nickname "Andros Glamour." She quickly loosed her bound-up, straight black hair that flowed past her shoulders. She was anxious to display her "Indian hair," as she called it, as a sign of authenticity. In Alma Miller's words:

> My family told me that in the slavery times, my foreparents were run away on a raft from Florida. And they come into Bahamas. They was my foreparents, great-grands . . . Alice and Isaac Miller [name listed in fig. 3]. But their first stop then was in Eleuthera. And one set had a family that stop by Cedar Coppitt [Andros], and therefore they make a home from there come through with the people and them Indian and whatever. And granddaddy went up in Eleuthera and they buy a lot a land up in there. And they come here [to Andros] and they buy a lot a land down here [in Lowe Sound] and about, in the swashes. [In] Eleuthera they open up a pineapple farm, and they had a sheep farm, and they had a beef farm up in Eleuthera. So the family scatter from Eleuthera and Andros and on South Andros. That's a wide wass of family of people. Some of the Millers still is in the States, you know. You come cross one or two of the family [there].
>
> My mommy told me that daddy [Edward Miller] use to tell them, say that when they goes to work in slavery time, they have a white boss, like the master. So they would go out and they work and they do all they master's work and sometime they be beaten. Then when they master beat them, they used to lay down on they belly, face down. The master used to beat them. Beat them good. They used to work for the masters. Mostly, say the old people tell when slavery began abolishing, then they begin running away on the raft to come to the Bahamas.
>
> Now them set what come over, I can't tell whether they been African or they's a pure blood of Indian. I know they was a Indian family, they was Indian blood. But just know when I be young and be traveling [in Florida] and the Indian they begin owning me, as a part of them. Sometime I see them right here in Nassau. They come over on trips and I go in the States the same thing. I go New York, the same thing, no different. Just when I buck one of them, they own me they hold me up.[27]

Charles Bowleg—Nicholls Town

Charles Bowleg, in his mid to late forties, lives in Nicholls Town and is readily identified by Bahamians as "Indian" because he is "bright" and has high cheekbones. He is a member of the Bowleg family that has long-established roots in Nicholls Town. His niece, Shelley Bowleg, is currently the principal of the Red Bays Primary School. Charles Bowleg told me that he learned the story of the Black Seminole exodus to the Bahamas from his grand aunt, Blossom Bowleg:

> She was Blossom Bowleg until she got married to Evans. Her parents came from the west coast of Andros. Her grandparents came from Florida, and they landed on the west coast at a place call Cedar Coppitt. And after a period of time, they was on the west coast, on the back side of Andros. It is very low so a hurricane came through, a very serious hurricane, and it wash out a lot of the land, and they were seeking for higher ground. So several of the younger ones, they get in these small boats, a canoe what they come over in, and they find a narrow passage which they call Bowleg Lake. The mouth of it enter in on the northeast side at Stafford Creek, and it goes in right straight through to the western part of the island. Big boats only can go halfway down through there because of the area. Some areas is so narrow and the water is so shallow and you go in about probably five miles and then the water's fresh. And the fresh water and the salt water at times pushes each other back and forth. So they use that as a channel to come through on the north side. Her grandparents told her that after they come over, they find on the north side was a much better place, higher ground. Then they went back and get the family, and come on the north side [Nicholls Town].
>
> After they came on the north side, they never went back. Blossom, Felix [are] brothers and sisters. Their father was one of the original people who came over [from the other side of Andros Island]. It was Simon and another one name Scipio, two brothers, Bowleg, and they the ones what come from the west. And then they migrate from there. They was mostly fishermens and farmers, and they sail all through the Bahamas and they left one or two here and there. So the family scatter out all through the Bahamas, but originally Bowlegs all from Nicholls Town. We have some in western Grand Bahama, and we have some in Eleuthera, but not a big amount. The big amount is in between Nassau and Freeport, west end.

I never knew my great-grandmother, I never recognize her name, but I heard she was mixed with Indian blood, light-skinned. Some [Bowlegs] were bright and some black. One of the sisters were medium brown, one of the sisters were bright. She was so bright they used to call her "Gold."

I used to go to Florida a lot when I was much younger and I run into several people who told me that they bears the same title [the Bowleg surname], even white ones. I run into a custom officer and he told me "You's a Bowleg?" I said, "Yeah." This other gentleman, his title was Bowleg. So he look at me, he say, "Oh, we got black ones too!" So he say, "And I see you from Andros." Say, "You know we are family?" So I say, "No, I don't know that." He said that most of his parents were Indians and they married white women, and that's how come he was white. But we have real bright girls and boys in our family, and some of them is real black. My mother was very bright and my daddy was light brown. But one thing is that they [Indians] never like boss man too much. The majority of them work for themselves, very short-temper. They rather fight one time and get it all over with. As far as the Indians is concern, they pretty peaceable until you get them out. Then they don't care about life anymore. That's the way it is.[28]

Omelia Marshall—Red Bays

At eighty years of age, Omelia Marshall, affectionately known as "Mama" or "Meena," or respectfully addressed as "Miss Marshall," is considered the matriarch of Red Bays. She is both revered and feared as a "bush medicine" woman. She still practices the bush medicine techniques taught to her by her father, Scipio Demeritte, but claims that she was forced to discontinue her midwifery practice because of threats from the Progressive Liberal Party (PLP) government, which ordered her to stop delivering babies or else go to jail. She blames this problem with the PLP administration on the fact that she has always been a member of the Free National Movement (FNM), which was the opposition party for twenty-five years in the Bahamas.

We met on numerous occasions in what she calls "Marshall Town," a compoundlike setting with several small houses and shacks set roughly in a circle—including a "tatch camp" that resembles a Seminole chickee—where she lives among three generations of family. Omelia Marshall relates:

The tatch camp built for hurricane. When the hurricane come down in Betsy Hurricane I had a big tatch camp [now only one small structure stands].

RH: So you're safer in the tatch camp than the house during a hurricane?

OM: Yes ma'am, [I] tell you something, if hurricane come now, and you got a tatch camp you go right in there, and you catch fire in that, make up your bed, then you go and get some cassava. You bake your bread you boil your hot coffee. You laying down sleeping, the wind blowing or what have you.[29]

The women of Marshall Town can be seen daily sewing baskets in the yard. Even a few of the small children sew too, proudly showing off their attempts at basketry. Mrs. Marshall's father, she says, was the first to start the basket-sewing tradition of Red Bays; he used sea grass and formed the baskets in one style—the fanner. She learned the craft from him, but improvised the style and materials.

Marshall Town is the main stop on tours of Red Bays, conducted mainly by staff from Forfar Field Station, who bring their students to hear "lectures" about Red Bays' history and culture from Mrs. Marshall.[30] For this service she received a plaque commending her outstanding "hospitality" from the Bahamas Tourism Board. She is very proud of this plaque and is quick to send one of the children to the house to retrieve it for viewing by visitors. Omelia Marshall remembers:

My great-granddaddy was Scipio Bowleg, and his son is Scipio Bowleg, and my daddy is Scipio Demeritte. My mother is Marion [Bowleg] Demeritte. She formerly from Red Bay, but my daddy from Lowe Sound. I come from Lowe Sound when I was nine years old, bathing in the sea, naked, nine years old. My grandmother name Marta Celeste Russell. My great-grandfather they say he leave from America Land where the Seminoles come from. Then when he come from there, he stop to Josie Cay [Joulter Cay]. From Josie Cay he leave from there and he go down to Cedar Coppitt and build he house. He kitchen and he house foundation still there.[31]

These oral traditions have been passed down through the older generations but, unfortunately, are rarely repeated to the children of contemporary Andros Island. The times when stories of their past were told around fires that lit the pitch-dark nights are gone; television entertainment and electric street lamps have replaced them for the younger generations.

Arrival of Black Seminoles

Already resident on Andros Island at the time of the Black Seminoles' arrival were British Loyalists—refugees from New York, the Carolinas, Georgia, and Florida[32]—who, along with their enslaved Africans, sought asylum in the Bahamas in 1783 after suffering defeat in the American Revolutionary War. The 1783 Treaty of Paris also required British Loyalists to leave San Andrés, an island off the Mosquito Coast of Latin America. Their arrival signaled substantial change in the social structure of the Bahamas, effectively doubling the population. The Loyalist refugee contingent also included "freed Negroes." During the Revolutionary War, the British military commander issued a proclamation promising freedom to all Africans who would join the British lines.[33] After the war, the faithful Africans received British-issued certificates of freedom, and many were subsequently permitted to live as free persons in the Bahamas. Others, not as fortunate, were sold by their Loyalist owners and reenslaved in Santo Domingo.

Another group who preceded the Black Seminoles' arrival on Andros Island was an undetermined number of "liberated Africans" who had been transported there after being rescued or liberated by the British Royal Navy from Spanish ships. These ships were intercepted en route to Cuba and other Spanish colonies where Africans were destined for enslavement. They intervened in the Spaniards' transport of Africans because the British had outlawed the slave trade in 1807. From 1811 to 1841 over 3,500 liberated Africans landed on New Providence. Some were relocated to various Out Islands, including Andros, but the majority of them remained on New Providence in Nassau, the capital city. The majority of liberated Africans were likely from the Congo and Angola regions, where the slave trade was concentrated during this period. On Andros, they settled mainly in the northeastern side of the island. Goggin records the following in a journal entry from Mastic Point, a northeastern Andros settlement:

> Journal entry July 17 [1937]: "Red Bay 'Indian people' did not associate much with the other blacks—Congo people—on the east side for a long time."

The presence of "Congos" in this area of Andros was reported by a naturalist who interviewed a Mastic Point woman "whose mother and father were full-blooded Congos."[34] Congos were also ostracized in Nassau, where fervent quarrels erupted among Africans from different ethnic groups.

Tensions also ran high in Nassau among white Bahamians, who were provoked to hostility by the presence of such a large number of Africans—free Africans who had never been enslaved. They were additionally alarmed by black troops of the 2nd West India Regiment who were stationed in the Bahamas.[35] Their fear was elevated due to the Haitian Revolution, which began in 1791, and the immigration of "French Negro" refugees from Saint Domingue, who in 1795 "concocted a plan to overthrow the government of the Bahamas, by seizing the ammunition at the forts, killing the inhabitants, destroying the town and liberating French prisoners. Discovery of the plot ended this plan. . . . The five perpetrators were arrested tried and convicted of treason in the General Court. . . . Only three were hanged as the other two were . . . sentenced to transportation out of the colony."[36]

Bahamian governor Sir J. Carmichael Smyth, a staunch abolitionist, attempted to ameliorate the brewing crisis by establishing several separate communities for the liberated Africans on the island of New Providence—the "African Villages" of Adelaide, Carmichael, and Gambier—situated far outside the city of Nassau.[37] Black Bahamian descendants of these liberated Africans claim a legacy of almost two hundred years of freedom.[38]

Long before any of the above groups arrived, however, Andros Island had earned the dubious reputation as a bastion of piracy. The island served as a strategic location from which pirates ambushed Spanish ships en route to Cuba.[39] In fact, the bay at the northernmost tip on Andros is named Morgan's Bluff, in honor of the infamous pirate Captain Henry Morgan. Piracy in the Bahamas was substantially thwarted, if not totally eliminated, after the arrival of Woodes Rogers, appointed as the first governor of the colony in 1718. His administration adopted the national motto *Expulsis Piratis Restituta Commercia* (Expel the Pirates, Restore Commerce).[40] Andros Island's reputation as a haven for illegal activities persists even today.

By choosing the remote, northwestern coast of Andros Island—an area covered with thick coppitts (Bahamian vernacular for "coppices," or densely wooded areas) and bordered by ship-deterring shallow waters—the Black Seminoles finally achieved the sanctuary and freedom they had so long sought. Not all of them, however, remained in this area that they christened "Red Bays." I was given two theories about the etymology of "Red Bays." Some say it is so named because of the reddish color of the sand; others say that the term "Red" refers to the Seminole Indians.

Some of the original Black Seminole refugees did not stop there, but continued traveling southeastwardly along the shoreline, scattering throughout Andros Island. They joined established settlements or founded new ones at several locations, including Nicholls Town,[41] Lowe Sound, Conch Bay, Mastic Point, Staniard Creek, Calabash Bay, Fresh Creek, and Mangrove Cay. Ironically, however, many members of these original settler families were eventually reunited in Red Bays over succeeding generations. Intermarriages frequently occurred between Red Bays' women and the men who traveled from other communities to North Andros for work, harvesting the fertile sponge beds of the Mud. After the sponge beds died in the 1930s, the men began cutting down the pineyard to make charcoal, a lucrative business. According to Marion Pickstock, a descendant of the original Black Seminole settlers: "The men liked this work better, they got money right in their hand. With sponging, [the] agent gave [them the] money later [after expenses in the truck and credit system]."[42] The population of Red Bays fluctuates between 260 to 280 people today.

Based upon the oral history and archival documents, Black Seminoles had been living as free men and women for seven years in the original settlement of Red Bays on the northwestern tip of Andros before their encounter with the British authorities. In June of 1828, Port of Nassau Searcher of Customs Winer Bethell seized and delivered to the port of Nassau via the sloop *Hannah and Susan* "thirty-two persons being black and persons of colour, alleging them to be slaves brought from Florida and illegally imported into Andros Island, one of the Bahama Islands."[43] Two months later, the Searcher of Customs issued another report with the names of "ninety-seven foreign Negro slaves," seized under similar circumstances as the former group, from Andros Island (see fig. 3).[44] Several names on this report match those names provided to me in the interviews with my consultants on Andros Island. This documentation confirms that their ancestors were among the original settlers who escaped from Florida.

The Slave Registration Act passed by the Bahamas legislature in 1821 possibly precipitated Bethell's "discovery" of the Black Seminoles on Andros Island. The institution of a triennial system of slave registration required slaveowners to submit a list of their slaves, indicating name, age, sex, complexion ("black" or "little yellow tinge" were common descriptions), place of employment, and birthplace ("African" or "Creole," that is, born in the West Indies). These slave registers date from 1821 to 1834, the year that slavery was abolished.[45] In an effort to prevent the indiscriminate transshipment of enslaved persons from island to island, this act required registration by "owners or persons licensed to export slaves from the . . . islands."[46] These "slave returns" exposed the fact that the Black Seminoles—whose presence was most likely well known to other Androsians because of trade and sponging activities—were conspicuously absent from these returns.

Bethell sincerely believed that he was saving them from certain enslavement: "I have thought it my duty to arrest and make seizure of them in order that they may pass through [a] competent court and being condemned to the Crown thereby bar any interest that might be set up by any person or persons whatever and so meeting what I conceive to be true and spiritual meaning and benevolent intentions of the act of Imperial Parliament passed prior to 5th George 4 ch. 113 for the abolition of the Slave Trade under which previous act I have seized said slaves."[47] Another government official, H. Twiss, concurred with Bethell's position on the matter, noting: "The fact that 97 Slaves were brought from Florida to the Bahamas seems indisputable. There may be direct and positive proof of the motives of the Importer, but in the absence of such proof, resort must be had to presumption and probabilities. If no rational motive can be assigned for bringing these Slaves to the Bahamas, except that of selling them into slavery in Cuba, and if, as the seizing officer states, the same practice has prevailed before, there would be enough, in the absence of any exculpatory evidence, to justify their condemnation to the Crown."[48]

Both of the 1828 customs reports indicated that the persons seized had been living on Andros Island since 1821, "peacefully and quietly, and have supported themselves upon fish, conchs and crabs which are to be met in abundance and upon Indian corn, plantains, yams, potatoes and peas which they have raised."[49] Although it was initially suspected that the Spanish had temporarily deposited them on Andros Island for eventual shipment to and enslavement in Cuba, further investigation revealed that this was not the case. These suspected "slaves" produced documents attesting to their support of the British in the War of 1812. It was also determined by the customs officers that all 97 of the people seized had come to the Bahamas on the same vessel. After reviewing the case, Bahamian governor Smyth remarked that "the question of these people being considered as slaves illegally imported was not noted until they had already been settled here seven years and that during these seven years, there did not occur a single instance of any one of these Negroes being carried away to Cuba. I see therefore no grounds to suspect any improper motives on the part of the owners of the vessels who brought them from Florida; or to doubt the truth of the story told by the poor people themselves more particularly as many of them still have their discharges from His Majesty's service."[50]

After almost one year of detention in Nassau, the Black Seminoles were released and returned to their homes in Red Bays, where they were subsequently permitted to live in freedom.[51] Their service in the British cause during the Revolutionary War, the War of 1812, and the British occupation of Florida from 1763 to 1783[52] was not the only reason for this latitude toward Africans in a colony where slavery yet remained an active policy. Indeed, there were several other important ones. First, to have done otherwise would have been contrary to the Consolidated Slave Act, part of which decreed that "persons arriving in any of His Majesty's colonies, from any foreign island or State where they were lawfully held in slavery cannot be sent back thither, or dealt with as slaves."[53] Second, slaveowners in the United States had been compensated for their loss of "property" by the British treaty adopted upon the conclusion of the War of 1812. They were paid "at the rate of £70 per head."[54] Finally, if these 97 people, designated as "slaves" in the reports, had been condemned to the Crown as seized property, "the Crown would be charged with the bounty of £7.10 per head,"[55] which would have amounted to a substantial expense for the colony. As Governor Smyth wrote:

> Not only [would] any legal process by which these Negroes could be condemned to the Crown as slaves illegally imported . . . be a very unnecessary expense, but that no further steps whatever are requisite for the establishment or maintenance of their freedom. These people have never been considered in the Colony as slaves and their names have never been entered on the slave registry. . . . I trust that if any doubt can be supposed to exist either in the minds of the Negroes themselves or if any of the planters on the neighboring islands as to these people being considered as Free British Subjects, the occasional and authorized visit of a clergyman of the Church of England in the discharge of his pastoral duties will completely remove them.[56]

After years of suffering, the Black Seminoles finally won their freedom—in the Bahamas.

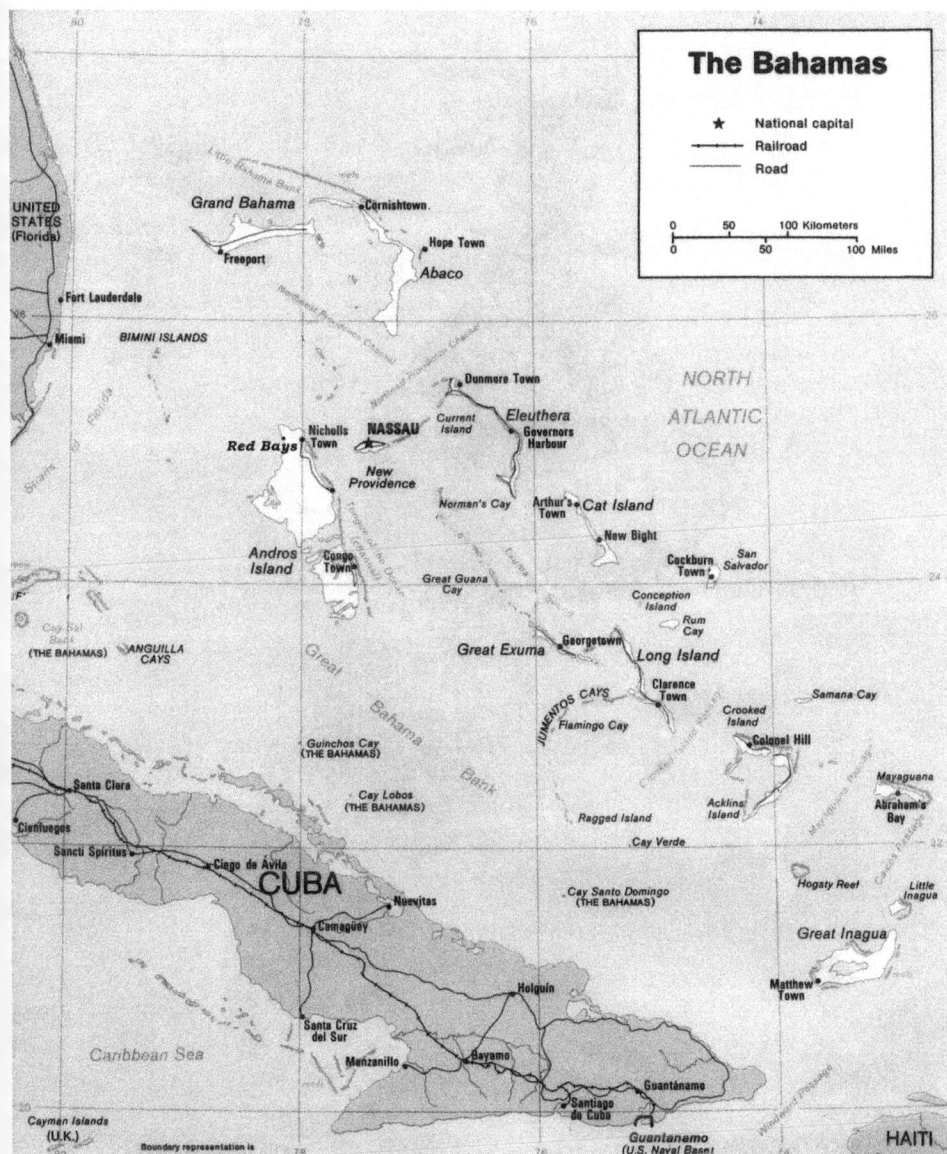

Map 1. The Bahamas

Map 2. Andros Island

Fig. 1. The Reverend Bertram A. Newton, 2000. Bertram A. Newton is the pastor of New Salem Baptist Church in Red Bays, retired teacher and principal of Red Bays Primary School, and author of a pamphlet entitled *A History of Red Bays, Andros, Bahamas.* He is pictured here in the church. He is the great-grandson of Moses Newton, one of the original Black Seminole settlers of Andros Island.

Fig. 2. Mrs. Omelia Marshall, 1997. Considered the matriarch of Red Bays, Mrs. Marshall is the granddaughter of Scipio Bowleg, a bush medicine doctor and original Black Seminole settler. She carries on the family tradition of bush medicine, is a retired midwife, and is the originator of the distinctive basket styles of Red Bays. At eighty-plus years old she still strips the palm thatch and sews baskets.

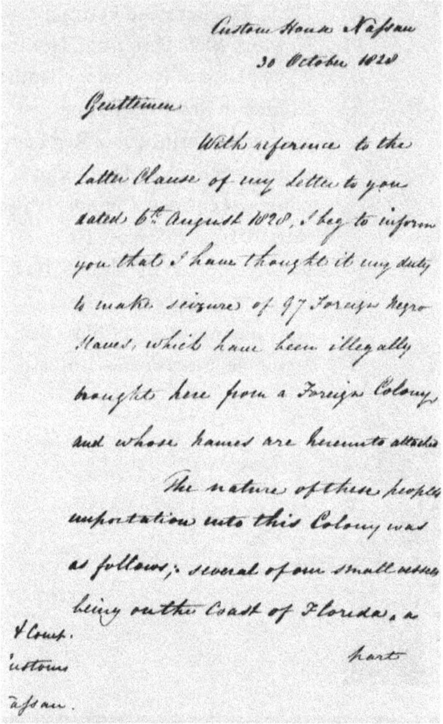

Custom House Nassau
30 October 1828

Gentlemen

With reference to the latter Clause of my Letter to you dated 6th August 1828, I beg to inform you that I have thought it my duty to make seizure of 97 Foreign Negro Slaves, which have been illegally brought here from a Foreign Colony, and whose names are hereunto attached.

The nature of these peoples importation into this Colony was as follows; several of our small vessels being on the Coast of Florida, a

& Comp.
Customs
Nassau.

part

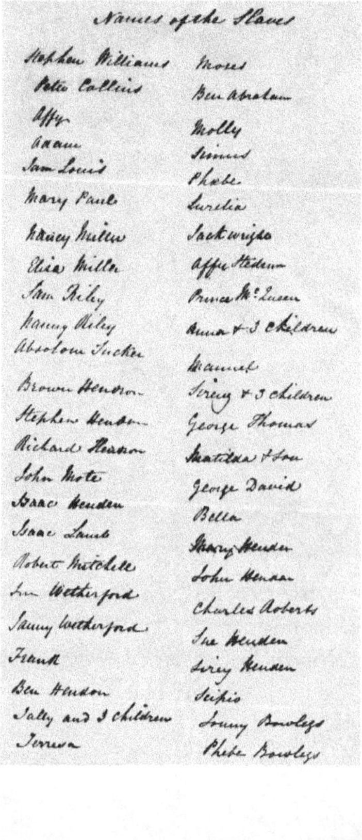

Names of the Slaves

Stephen Williams	Moses
Peter Collins	Ben Abraham
Affy	Molly
Adam	Simmons
Sam Louis	Phebe
Mary Paul	Lucretia
Nancy Miller	Jack wright
Eliza Miller	Affe Stedman
Sam Riley	Prince McQueen
Nancy Riley	Anna & 3 Children
Absolom Tucker	Manuel
Brown Henderson	Sirey & 3 children
Stephen Henderson	George Thomas
Richard Henderson	Matilda & Son
John Mote	George David
Isaac Henden	Bella
Isaac Lamb	Mary Henden
Robert Mitchell	John Henden
Sam Wetherford	Charles Roberts
Sammy Wetherford	Sue Henden
Frank	Sirey Henden
Ben Henson	Scipio
Sally and 3 children	Sonny Bowlegs
Teresa	Phebe Bowlegs

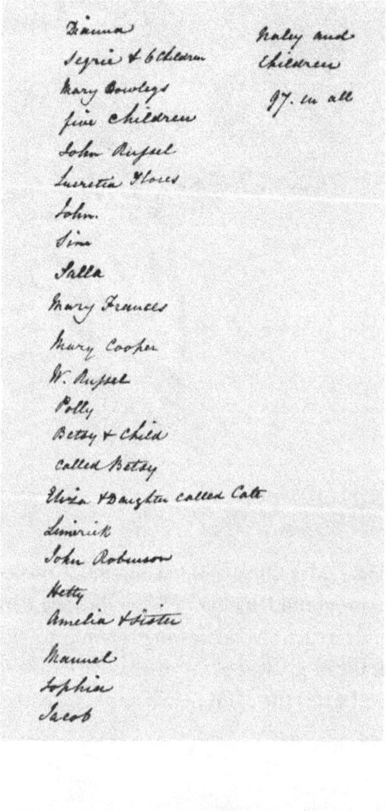

Dianna
Sugrie & 6 Children
Mary Bowlegs
five Children
John Russel
Lucretia Flores
John
Sina
Sally
Mary Frances
Mary Cooper
W. Russel
Polly
Betsy & Child
called Betsy
Eliza & Daughter called Cate
Limerick
John Robinson
Hetty
Amelia & Sister
Manuel
Sophia
Jacob

Nelly and Children

97. in all

Fig. 3a. (*left*). October 30, 1828, letter from customs officer W. Bethell reporting the seizure of "97 Foreign Negro Slaves" (first page of letter).

Fig. 3b. (*bottom left*). First page of the "Names of Slaves" list attached to the letter of October 30, 1828.

Fig. 3c. (*bottom right*). Second page of the "Names of Slaves" list.

Fig. 4. The Reverend Frederick Russell, 1997. Frederick Russell, who died in 1999, was associate pastor of New Salem Baptist Church in Red Bays before becoming the pastor of Mizpah Baptist Church in Nicholls Town, Andros Island. Born in Red Bays, he spent much of his life in Nassau as a licensed practical nurse at Princess Margaret Hospital. He is the great-grandson of John Russell, a Black Seminole settler.

Fig. 5. The Reverend Benjamin Lewis, 1996. Benjamin Lewis is the great-grandson of Sammy Lewis, one of the original Black Seminole settlers in Red Bays (listed in the customs roster as "Sam Louis"). Currently serving as the associate pastor of New Salem Baptist Church in Red Bays, he is a retired carpenter and seaman.

Fig. 6. Sisters Mary Russell (left) and Alma "Prudence" Miller, 1997. Mary Russell and Prudence Miller are the great-granddaughters of Alice and Issac Miller, who were among the original Black Seminole settlers from Florida, and who settled in Lowe Sound, where both women continue to reside.

Fig. 7. William "Scrap Iron"/ "Old Iron" Colebrooke, 2000. Old Iron Colebrooke is one of the few men in Red Bays who sews baskets. He was a seaman before losing his boat. He is the grandson of William Colebrooke, a Black Seminole settler from Florida. He is pictured here with Daisy Jumper, a member of the Seminole Tribe of Florida.

Fig. 8. Daisy Jumper, 2000. Daisy is a full-blood Red Stick Seminole Indian and member of the Seminole Tribe of Florida. She is the great-granddaughter of Chief Jumper, who fought in the Seminole Wars. Daisy is standing in front of a "thatch camp" in Mrs. Omelia Marshall's compound in Red Bays. This structure resembles the Seminole chickee.

Fig. 9. Charles Bowleg, 1997. Charles is a seaman and utility company worker in Nicholls Town, Andros Island. His surname is the only one remaining among the Black Seminole settlers in the Bahamas that is directly tied to the Florida Seminoles (e.g., Chief Billy Bowlegs).

Fig. 10. Palm "top." Cut from the pineyards surrounding Red Bays, a palm top is hung to dry on a clothesline. When dry, it is stripped and sewn into baskets. The earlier baskets were made from sea grass. Mrs. Omelia Marshall innovated the use of silver palm top as an alternative material.

Fig. 11. Red Bays baskets. The art of basket weaving has been passed down through the generations among residents of Red Bays. The distinctive construction and styles of these baskets are unique to these Black Seminole descendants in Red Bays, and are very different from "straw work" in other areas of the Bahamas.

Fig. 12. New Salem Baptist Church

Fig. 13. Red Bays Primary School

Fig. 14. Man placing sponges on the shore to dry. Sponging was a major factor in the Bahamian economy until the mid 1930s, when a mysterious bacterium or fungus attacked the sponge beds. Sponging is one of the subsistence strategies in Red Bays.

Fig. 15. Sign announcing the entrance into Red Bays. For motorists traveling from elsewhere on the Andros Island, this sign is the first indication of the settlement, which is located at the end of a twenty-mile road.

Fig. 16. An area called "the bay." This is the dock where Red Bays seamen anchor their fishing boats.

Fig. 17. Crab pen. During the rainy season, the crabs "walk" and are caught and placed in these pens, where they are fattened up for later sale.

Fig. 18. Mahogany carving by Red Bays woodcarver Henry Wallace. Henry Wallace had a one-man show at George Mason University and has demonstrated his craft at the Smithsonian Institution.

In ones and twos, in their dugout
canoes, the Negro Seminoles crossed
the Gulf Stream and landed along the
western shore of Andros from the
Joulter Cays south over a twenty-year
period. They congregated at Red Bays.

The Reverend Bertram A. Newton

4 ✐

"We Reach"

Bahamaland

In Bahamian dialect, *to reach* is used intransitively to mean to arrive at a destination. Having survived the treachery of enslavement, persistent pursuit by
slave catchers, marronage among the indigenous peoples of Florida, and the
perilous journey across the Gulf Stream—many traveling in dugout canoes—
the Black Seminoles of Florida finally *reached*: they arrived at the "Promised
Island" and freedom in the Bahamas.

The Commonwealth of the Bahamas, or "Bahamaland,"[1] is an archipelago,
consisting of 700 islands—only 32 of which are inhabited—and 2,400 cays and
rocks that stretch from the southeastern coast of Florida eastward toward the
Windward Passage north of Cuba and Haiti. Early-sixteenth-century archaeological and historical literatures provide evidence of a substantial Lucayan settlement on the east coast of Andros, and that contact between Lucayans and
indigenous Floridians had been established.[2] During the early colonial era, the
Spanish, French, and British intermittently claimed possession of the Bahamas.
The British ultimately gained nominal control in 1670, but did not establish
any systematic government for almost fifty years, and during that period, the

French and Spanish took advantage of the situation; both groups "plundered the colony, and [drove] out the few English settlers."[3] In 1718 the British dispatched Woodes Rogers, who would become the Bahamas' first governor, to suppress the rampant piracy besieging the colony. Pirates had long established the Bahamas—and Andros Island in particular, because of its proximity to the Florida coast—as a supreme location from which to prey on Spanish ships sailing through the Straits of Florida.[4]

Social Landscapes

Beginning in 1783, the sociopolitical and sociocultural landscapes of the Bahamas were significantly transformed by the arrival of the Loyalists and their enslaved Africans, many of whom were creoles. Before the Loyalists arrived, "only a few of the Bahama islands were inhabited. The more densely populated islands were New Providence [Nassau], Eleuthera, and Harbour Island. A few people were scattered on Exuma, Long Island, Cat Island and the Turks and Caicos Islands. The total population of these islands was estimated to be about 4,002."[5] Loyalists were of two classes: the first group were "farmers who settled on the Out Islands with large families and ten, twenty or a hundred slaves, and the second group ... were officers, merchants and professionals, many of whom wished to return to America when conditions settled down."[6]

Some Loyalists and their contingents settled on New Providence but the majority settled on Bahamian Out Islands, including Abaco (the most widely advertised to the Loyalist settlers),[7] Eleuthera, Exuma, Cat Island, Long Island, Acklins, Crooked Island, San Salvador (then called Watlings Island), and Turks and Caicos (then part of the Bahamas).[8] Their arrival virtually doubled the size of the white Bahamian population and tripled the black population. In 1787 Andros became the sanctuary for approximately 1,400 Loyalists refugees from North America and Central America. They substantially altered the population there. The total number of enslaved persons on Andros, and planters owning ten or more of them, more than doubled upon their arrival.[9]

Loyalists received land grants and attempted to reestablish the plantation culture and economy that they had long enjoyed in the North American South and in Central America. These efforts failed miserably, due to the unsuitability of the rocky land, unyielding soil, and devastation caused by the chenille bug that between 1788 and 1794 "destroyed hundreds of tons of cotton and nearly bankrupted the American Loyalists. Consequently with their finances nearly exhausted many of the Loyalists sold their land, took their slaves and returned to America."[10]

The large influx of liberated Africans, freed from Spanish slave ships after 1807, alarmed the white Bahamian population. Their response was the enactment of strict laws that prohibited integrated housing, and "demanded that all people of colour be off the streets of the town of Nassau after 9:00 P.M. when the Town Bell rang."[11] Similar laws were enacted on the Out Islands, although they were not as restrictive, owing to the substantial differences in lifestyles as compared to Nassau. These laws nevertheless had the effect of creating and codifying new racial barriers.

By the time the Black Seminoles arrived in 1821, there was an established hierarchical social structure in the Bahamas that was similar to but varied in important ways from the system in the United States. In the Bahamas there was "hope" of rising above one's ascribed racial category and achieving a higher status in the racial hierarchy. Vertical status mobility was made possible by a Loyalist-inspired act that adjudged "any one above three degrees removed in a lineal descent from the Negro ancestor was to be considered white."[12] This had relatively no impact on the Black Seminoles, however, who chose to remain virtually isolated in northwestern Andros Island for almost 150 years. The entire island was sparsely populated and remains so today.

The Bahamas has historically suffered from scarcity of natural resources, widely dispersed population, epidemics, and vast destruction wrought by hurricanes and by wars among European powers vying for control of the country. These exigencies created a scenario wherein all Bahamians were integral to achieving the colony's viability, which explains to some degree why the institution of slavery there varied from the form that was manifested in other West Indian countries.

The Bahamas' positioning in the complex legacy of slavery and colonialism in the Caribbean region is extraordinary. The experiences of African peoples there deviated from the norm of West Indian plantation life in several ways. First, there was the presence of a large number of Africans who had been "liberated" by the British from slave ships en route to Spanish colonies after the British abolished the slave trade. These liberated Africans were not actually freed upon arriving in British territory. As subjects of open-ended indentureships, the experience for most was merely a different form of slavery. Some among the British colonizers were apparently sympathetic to the plight of these apprenticed Africans. This attitude is clearly evident in some of the records of that era, and is aptly illustrated in the following Governor's Despatch, which deserves duplication almost in its entirety.

[I] am unwilling to believe in the intuition of the Governor again to assign over to Masters those persons who had completed periods of apprenticeship, some of them upwards of 14 years and none of them under seven, and who, as appears in the course of the investigation now proceeding with, had given the most decided proofs of their being able to provide for themselves in the absolute fact that, for many years of their apprenticeship and some of them for the whole period, they had been left by their holders not only to do this but in addition to pay to the holders considerable weekly or monthly sums. The average of the sums so paid by the able-bodied Africans appears in general to have been about six dollars per month. Sailors paid more and the holders took no further notice of them than to receive this money, and to find employment for them in cases where they did not find it for themselves. There may exist reason to doubt whether the industry of these persons would continue equally steady if no demand was made upon the fruits of it. . . . I willingly allow the full forces of this doubt and the propriety of being guided by it, but it appears to me that after the completion of one period of apprenticeship, industry should be converted to the interest of the African ultimately, and not to that of an individual who had no sort of other regard for him. . . . [H]aving thus ascertained that the African has been industrious, there will be returned to him said portion of the sum as may appear at the time amply sufficient for his immediate reasonable purposes and the surplus deposited with a savings bank to be afterwards issued to him where and how it may be done best to his advantage. Many of the forfeited Africans are connubially connected with slaves and have affinities by them. . . . They suggested the purchase of their connections might perhaps be brought about. Respectfully submitting what I have stated, I beg to leave to repeat the question "Whether it is the intention of the Order in council of 19th July 1825 that those Africans who have already completed full periods of apprenticeship should again be liable to be assigned by the Collector to other persons for a period not exceeding seven years?"

I have the honour to be with respect
My Lord
Lewis Grant (Major General, Governor)[13]

This communiqué illustrates a remarkable concern for the welfare of Africans in the Bahamas, one that increasingly resonated throughout the British West Indies during this period. The concern reached a crescendo in 1834 when the institution was finally ended by the Abolition Act of February 15.[14] In July 1834, Governor Balfour issued a proclamation to those soon to become ex-masters and ex-slaves, admonishing them "to treat the apprentices properly and humanely and the slaves to act in a respectful manner as would befit their new status."[15] There was, however, an additional four-year period of "apprenticeship" imposed by the act that amounted to four more years of free or substantially free labor for white Bahamians.

Governor J. Carmichael Smyth, a staunch abolitionist who became governor in 1829, was the subject of much concern among white Bahamians. Not only did Smyth advocate for the amelioration of conditions for the enslaved, abolition of corporal punishment for enslaved females, and elimination of slavery, but, acting under the king's instructions, he called for equal black representation as jurors. These and other actions caused significant angst among white Bahamians; his demise as colonial governor is largely attributed to these very issues.[16]

Another way that the institution of slavery was different in the Bahamas was that, in contrast to most of the British West Indies, many Bahamian plantation-owners were residents. They or their overseers demonstrated less proclivity toward physical violence against the enslaved, and were "more concerned with the preservation of their capital [slaves were "property"] and less with meeting production targets than hired overseers might have been."[17] A third distinguishing factor was geography. Large-scale agriculture—such as that practiced in other British colonies—was attempted, but eventually abandoned; the lack of topsoil on most islands made it virtually impossible. These experiential differences have led to a perception by some scholars that the Bahamian colonial experience was benevolent in comparison to that of the rest of the West Indies. This, I suggest, is a misperception, one that has been responsible for the relative absence of the Bahamas in much of the research and literature on slavery and colonialism in the circum-Caribbean region. While Africans enslaved there did escape the ravages of "sweet power,"[18] which defined many West Indian economics, the socialization of slavery and colonialism in the Bahamas was nonetheless physically, psychologically, and culturally destructive.[19] The "structures and dynamics of racial inequality"[20] that manifested in colonial Bahamas are similar to those found in other parts of the West Indies and the African diaspora in general.

"One God, One People, One Bahamas"

People of African descent constitute the vast majority of the contemporary Bahamian population, and distinctions are often made between "black" and "white" Bahamians by Bahamians themselves. The black-white binary racial paradigm prevalent in the United States also operates in modern Bahamian society, but with some interesting nuances. White or "pass-as-white" Bahamians, currently numbering about 15 percent of the population, are divided into three subclasses: (1) the Bay Street Boys and Conchy Joes, (2) poor, semiliterate whites, and (3) Family Island whites. The Bay Street Boys and Conchy Joes largely inherit their wealth and emulate the lifestyles of former British administrators as much as possible under a black government. The term *Bay Street Boys* refers to the white merchants and lawyers. *Conchy Joes* is a term for those whose families were not among the elite class of "white" Bahamians; they are are often just hardworking fishermen and spongers, whose ancestors resided in the Bahamas before the arrival of the aristocratic Loyalists in the late eighteenth century. Family Island whites are those who, though isolated and undereducated, live moderately comfortable lifestyles by dominating the boating, fishing, and cottage tourism industries on their islands.[21] Those Bahamians who "pass as white" actually have what is termed in Bahamian dialect a "lick-o'-de-brush,"[22] but the principle of hypodescent[23] does not operate as stringently here as it does in the United States. Among black Bahamians, however, there is a hierarchy based upon phenotype, primarily skin color. The light-skinned, or "bright," people have traditionally been viewed as more attractive and have often enjoyed better opportunities than their darker-skinned brethren as a result. This hierarchical tradition began during the days of slavery, when distinctions were made within the free-people-of-color group between "free blacks" and "free coloureds."[24]

Abaco is popularly known as the "white island" because its eight-thousand-person population is approximately 50 percent white, a higher proportion than any other island in the Bahamas. The island's highly developed infrastructure and large resort areas make it one of the wealthiest, where conditions are arguably better than on any other island excluding, perhaps, the tourist meccas of New Providence and Grand Bahama. The obviously disparate wealth and power of Abaconians versus other Family Islanders raises the question: Is race a factor? The former prime minister is an Abaconian, and the history of blacks on Abaco would seem to explicate Mr. Ingraham's wider acceptance among whites.

When blacks gained control of the government in 1967, whites from the island of Abaco grumbled loudly about the new policies. They did not want to be subjected to the authority of what they considered was a hostile, racist, and incompetent black government in Nassau; other opponents included black Bahamians who had accumulated wealth in Abaco and viewed an alliance with Abaconian whites as their best strategy. They formed several organizations—the Greater Abaco Council (GAC), the Friends of Abaco (FOA), and the Abaco Independence Movement (AIM)—to launch activities designed to exempt themselves from the government's control. Petitions for secession and, later, designation as a separate country were rejected by the British government and the Bahamian House of Assembly, respectively. Abaconians finally resigned themselves to the inevitability of black Bahamian governance. In the words of Errington Watkins, a leader of the United Bahamian Party (UBP): "We have no other choice at this stage but to go along with an independent Bahamas. I don't mean we must join the PLP [Progressive Liberal Party]—God forbid—but we must do everything we can to make Abaco a success in an independent Bahamas."[25]

Another area of the Bahamas that has historically been dominated by white Bahamians is the settlement of Spanish Wells, located on the island of Eleuthera. Black Bahamians are excluded from the settlement, except as domestic workers who are forced to leave before dusk each day. Spanish Wells residents are reputedly so averse to "race-mixing" that they remain endogamous, to the point of close relative interbreeding. Consequently, it has earned a reputation as a place where one would readily find the products of such dangerous incestual encounters. Amelia Defries, a self-described white "adventurer" in the Bahamas relates this story:

> The Bishop, in Nassau, prevented my going to one island [Spanish Wells] where I had hoped to study white degeneracy. He told me I might lose my reason if I went there and ought not to tax endurance to such a point. It is an island where English people tried to keep free from mixing with the black race. Inbreeding has caused the most frightful degeneration, and at almost

every window idiots gape. The *Baltimore Expedition* published photos of most terrible examples—men with three eyes, women with seven fingers, and so on—fearful to see. The black folk, with Nature's wisdom usually sail away to far islands in their search for a mate.[26]

The veracity of this oft-repeated story is questionable. However, Spanish Wellians' proclivity for "racial" exclusivity is without doubt.

Andros Island, on the other hand, has historically been the province of black Bahamians. A small number of whites live there, but the overwhelming majority—approximately 95 percent—of the eight thousand Androsians are of predominantly African descent and are phenotypically "black." The traditional livelihood strategies there include fishing, farming, crabbing, and sponging. Several small fishing and diving resorts are the island's only claim to any type of tourist activity. The lack of resorts is largely due to the extremely limited infrastructure on the island. In the early years of the black majority PLP administration, Andros underwent vast changes with the introduction of electricity, running water, roads, and, very importantly, an increase in the number of schools and teachers. These changes however were at a minimal level, and once accomplished, they were rarely augmented. Although South Andros was represented by former prime minister Sir Lynden Pindling, the island did not flourish under his twenty-five-year tenure in office. It remained a "Sleeping Giant"; its natural and human resources latent. This increases an outside observer's surprise at the enigmatic loyalty that Androsians have traditionally proffered the PLP.

Political Maturation of Black Bahamians

Loyalists criticized the government extant in the Bahamas upon their arrival. Conchs (white inhabitants who had been resident for a long time) and colonial administrators were significantly outnumbered by the Loyalists; their leadership finally succumbed to the Loyalists' numerical strength and mounting representation in the House of Assembly.[27] In Britain, the Imperial Act for the Abolition of the Slave Trade was passed in 1807, and free blacks were afforded the right of suffrage in the Bahamas. Most, however, could not exercise this right because of a land-ownership requirement. Black Bahamians, though keenly interested in the elections, were unquestionably ignorant of the actual political process, a condition that sustained the hegemony of the Bay Street Boys.

The "art of political organization"[28] came slowly to black Bahamians. The wave of protests and riots that swept over most of the West Indian colonies in the 1930s bypassed the Bahamas because the black majority was hesitant to challenge the white establishment. Other factors contributed to the slow development of group consciousness among black Bahamians, and "ranked highly among these were: their aspirations to be white, deep divisions between assimilated and unassimilated free coloured, and the persistence of racial distinction within the free coloured population that continued until Emancipation."[29]

Tensions in the Bahamas climaxed in 1942 and 1958, when labor disputes escalated into strikes. Both of these occasions of civil unrest were attributed to the culmination of class and race hatred and marked the beginning of organized protest.[30]

The 1950s and 1960s marked a period of unprecedented political activity in the Bahamas. The black majority formed the first Bahamian political party in 1953: the PLP. The PLP was initially ridiculed by white Bahamians as the "Negro Communist Party." Just five years later, however, the Bay Street Boys recognized the serious threat the PLP had become to their entrenched political dominance, and fearing an erosion of their power, they decided to organize the UBP. Immediately the UBP attempted to gerrymander electoral boundaries and sought to delay woman suffrage, which would have effectively doubled the size of the black electorate.[31]

The redistricting act of 1967 provided the vehicle by which the black majority finally gained control of the government; PLP leader Lynden Pindling was elected as the first black Bahamian prime minister. Independent status in the British Commonwealth was achieved on July 10, 1973. These accomplishments were the culmination of years of increasing political awareness and pressure by the majority black Bahamian populace.

Historically, black Bahamians played insignificant roles in the political and economic affairs of the country. For centuries, the colony was administered by British bureaucrats, but it was the economic and political power of the Bay Street Boys, the white merchants and lawyers, that effectively controlled the Bahamas before independence. Although much change has occurred—black faces have dominated the political front lines since the late 1960s—white Bahamian money continues to wield significant power in Bahamian society. This was the case even during the PLP reign and its restrictive economic policy of "Bahamianisation."

This same argument of disproportionate white Bahamian influence is advanced, vociferously, against the Free National Movement (FNM) government. Critics charge that the FNM is a puppet of the white Bahamian power structure because a group of former UBP members—the Bay Street Boys—were among its founders. The other founders of the FNM were former PLP members who were dissatisfied with Pindling's leadership. These disgruntled PLPs split to form the "Free PLP," and later joined former UBP members to establish the FNM Party. Further, critics suggest that the FNM policy of "Globalisation" serves to benefit the "haves" rather than the "have-nots." Paradoxically, a majority of the black middle class, primary beneficiaries of the PLPs "Bahamianisation" policies, are now solidly in the FNM camp.

Progressive Liberal Party

PLP leader Lynden Pindling was elected prime minister in 1967, the first black Bahamian to ever lead the country. After gaining control of the government, the PLP rallied the masses of black Bahamians under the banner of "Bahamianisation." The explicit political goal of this policy was to give black Bahamians preferential access to employment and ownership opportunities in business and industry. Its sociocultural goal was to elevate black Bahamians' self-image, and their sense of pride that had been submerged beneath centuries of colonization and exploitation. A heightened sense of self-esteem would, ostensibly, flow from the economic empowerment induced by Bahamianisation. These policies had both dramatic successes and failures.

Governmental encouragement of Bahamian entrepreneurship became problematic because most Bahamians who purchased businesses and real estate did not have a firm capital base and, therefore, incurred substantial bank debt that limited growth potential. This scenario resulted in the creation of few jobs and the loss of many. Unemployment rates rose dramatically; from virtually 0 percent in the 1960s (colonial days) to 25 percent in 1983 (independent black Bahamian leadership).[32]

Bahamianisation policies did succeed in creating a new black middle class. Ironically, however, an unforeseen consequence of Bahamianisation was the marginalization of the masses of people who were most victimized by the racial discrimination of the past, and who had been the PLP's strongest supporters. Policy detractors argued that Bahamianisation "looked outwards to cut back external intervention in and control over the Bahamian economy rather than inwards to redistribute wealth or power within the existing Bahamian society. In sum it was archetypical of the nationalist bourgeoisie approach to the needs of a small polity/economy/society."[33] The result of this approach was "essentially a replacement of the political, social, and economic hegemony of a white bourgeoisie by a hegemony of a black bourgeoisie that is complete in the political sector, largely complete in the social sector, but still incomplete in the economic sector, where the white bourgeoisie retains a predominant share."[34]

The sense of continuity garnered during the twenty-five-year rule of the PLP government certainly fostered stability, but it also sowed the seeds of complacency and corruption in the Bahamas. The PLP administration was plagued by drug-related scandals and fluctuating economic cycles closely tied to events in the United States.[35] In the early 1980s, illicit drug trafficking produced great wealth, some of which found its way into legitimate investments. Cash from the drug trade fueled the growth of the banking industry and led to the creation of what has been termed a "false economy." Compounding matters for the PLP government, the United States took a strong position in the 1980s alleging Bahamian government involvement in the drug trade. This helped to damage the image of the Bahamas and led to a precipitous decline in tourism—its prime industry—and a concomitant rise in unemployment rates.

Free National Movement

The FNM, governing party of the Bahamas, was led by Prime Minister Hubert Ingraham until the March 2002 elections, at which time PLP candidate Perry Christie was elected the new prime minister. The FNM had wrenched power from the PLP in the 1992 general election, and its candidates were highly successful in the March 1997 general election, which was held while I was resident in the Bahamas conducting research. The divisive nature of Bahamian politics became quite evident during the campaign, and revealed complex sociocultural dynamics on a national level, as well as among the residents of Red Bays, the settlement where I resided. I was struck by the intensity of emotions displayed during the election process. I discovered that national politics are more significant to the average Bahamian than to voters in the United States because, unlike in the United States, where there are primary elections as well as general elections, the sole opportunity to voice an opinion on the candidates in the Bahamas is in a general election.

Bahamian elections have always been reputed as "rough and rumbustious" affairs,[36] but the general election of 1997 established an unfortunate new benchmark when a FNM member of Parliament was slain by men alleged to have been pro-PLP gang members. Political battles have been customarily limited to verbal sparring. Vindictive personal criticism, character defamation, and accusations of clientalism are typically "sandwiched in between lengthy quotations from or allusions to the Bible, for no party in the Bahamas will ever come to power unless leaders are seen as Christians."[37]

Politicians of both parties skillfully employ the use of biblical imagery, an established feature of Bahamian political debate. Former prime minister Lynden Pindling has been portrayed as Moses, the savior-hero-leader, who symbolically led his people from Egypt (that is, a white-controlled, colonized state) to the promised land of majority rule.[38] Likewise, the FNM subscribes to religious symbolism, as evinced in its motto: "Forward, Upward, Onward, Together, with God as our Beacon, our Leader and our Rock."[39]

Pindling's death in the year 2000 presented a critical juncture for the PLP. Lacking his strong and seasoned guidance—even from the sidelines, to which he had been forced after the 1997 election, when he lost his seat in the House of Assembly—the PLP leadership was in a major transition. The FNM was faced with massive disenchantment among the Bahamian people and new opposition in the 2002 election from other political parties that have gained increasing recognition and support from the black Bahamian populace.

The FNM government has extended much latitude to external capital investment. This may eventually cause an erosion of sovereignty, a context that emerges as a result of asymmetrical power relations extant between the Bahamas and more economically powerful countries such as the superpower United States. This asymmetry, unfortunately, is an undeniable reality for most Caribbean countries, not only the Bahamas. As Anthony P. Maingot suggests, "most claims to reciprocity and equivalence in today's international relations are in fact . . . rhetorical facades hiding gross or subtle domination and exploitation."[40]

The 1997 General Election

The Black Seminole descendants of Red Bays were historically peripheral actors in politics, but after independence in 1973 they developed intense allegiances to one of two parties. For thirty years, the PLP could bank on most Androsians' party loyalty. Former prime minister Sir Lynden Pindling—who led the PLP throughout its twenty-five-year reign in government—had been the representative to Parliament for South Andros, although he was born and raised in New Providence. In 1992 the political air was thick with rumors of governmental corruption, drug scandals, and high unemployment rates, all of which served to catapult the FNM into power. After their defeat in 1992, the PLP still maintained a respectable number of seats in the House of Assembly, and it continued to dominate the Family Island voters, including Androsians. In its 1997 general election victory, however, the FNM claimed thirty-five of forty seats in the House of Assembly, including all of the Family Island seats formerly held by the PLP. The FNM sweep was a clear mandate from marginalized Bahamians, who voted to stake their hopes for a better future in the FNM.

The Election: Through the Lens of Red Bays

The FNM campaign rally, at the North Andros High School track field in Nicholls Town, drew many residents of Red Bays; it was an "event." The school bus, which daily carried Red Bays children to this same location, became a campaign bus for this night. Speakers strained to have their voices heard above the clamor of the crowd chanting "Better, Better, going to get Better," the FNM campaign theme, to the blare of calypso music. Each speaker was escorted to the stage with a procession of dancing and cheering supporters. When the crowd calmed down, the candidate for member of Parliament in North Andros, Dr. Earl Deveaux, and Prime Minister Ingraham advanced their platforms.

The prime minister seized this opportunity to mention the Andros Islanders' historically loyal PLP voting record, warning that if they did not join in the FNM majority, their island would be left out of the FNM Manifesto, an elaborate plan to make life "Better, Better" in the Bahamas. This point projected clearly as he admonished them, "You make your bed hard, you lie in it hard."[41] This message reverberated throughout Red Bays for days afterward. Undaunted, loyal PLP supporters brushed off the clearly threatening tone of Ingraham's remark by saying that "Red Bays people like a hard bed." FNM supporters, however, used it to persuade the undecided to cast their votes for the FNM, pointing out that for progress to occur in Red Bays, they must join the winning team. Preelection polls were indicating another clear victory for the incumbent FNM prime minister. Nevertheless, some hard-line PLP supporters simply refused to enter the fold; it was, understandably, difficult for them to believe that their party, which had ruled for so long, could possibly lose once again. The strongest PLP supporters were those people who had obviously benefited from PLP policies and favoritism in the past. PLP members owned both of the "shops" (small stores stocking a limited line of groceries) in Red Bays, and they were the local government representatives. This status gave them a substantial amount of control over fund allocation and, therefore, control over the lives of many in this small community. The fact that many people in this rural settlement are illiterate increased their vulnerability to the various "spins" supplied by literate folk—of both political persuasions—to the campaign rhetoric and literature.

Riders to the PLP campaign rally held at a later date but at the same high school auditorium were served by pickup truck, not the school bus, because the school bus driver was "an FNM." The rally's featured speaker was none other than former prime minister Lynden O. Pindling. The crowd greeted him with wild cheers. Suffering from prostate cancer, he appeared frail, but his message was still powerful. He was "preaching to the choir" as he denounced the FNM's pro-privatization stance and its elimination of nine seats in the House of Assembly, a strategic move that severely impacted the PLP power base. Several other speakers criticized the FNM candidate, Dr. Earl Deveaux, for his lack of historical residence on Andros and signified about his "white wife." While they agreed with the FNM's proposal to make Andros the "breadbasket of the Bahamas" through new farming initiatives, they also supported the introduction of assembly plants for light industry.[42] The crowd reacted much more favorably to the suggestion of manufacturing and tourism industries than the farming initiative. Farming is viewed by most Androsians as too labor-intensive and low-status: "it's a job for Haitians."

Party rivalries among Red Bays residents escalated as the campaign wore on. Accusations of corruption and payoffs on both sides wrought angry confrontations between friends and family members. One PLP supporter threatened his sons and daughters with eviction from their home if they did not vote his party preference. The school bus driver, a staunch FNM supporter, raised the ire of many residents when he refused to pick up their children at the usual bus stop, which happened to be in the yard of a PLP supporter. Sisters fell out, no longer visiting with or "hailing" one another, and neighbors were "ravving" each other. Serious rifts were created which did not heal until months after the election. Yet while the voters were on a collision course, election fever running high, the candidates for the House of Assembly were rather friendly rivals. While one candidate offered his opponent a lunch after the campaign was over, the other candidate pledged a bottle of champagne. The ironies of politics.

On election day, the Red Bays Primary School became a polling place, and most of the eligible voters in Red Bays lined up at 9:00 A.M. sharp to cast their votes. Sporting the T-shirts designed with logos of the PLP or FNM, they filed in a few at a time, returning to the dirt yard outside with broad smiles and blackened thumbs, marred by the ink required as a precaution against voter fraud. Milling around outside the polling place were most of the men from the settlement, drunk with election fervor and Green Seal rum. Some drove around Red Bays, honking horns on their cars, which were heavily tattooed with bumper stickers.

ZNS, the Bahamian national radio station, broadcast the election results later that night; Red Bays residents listened anxiously for word of their candidate's standing, lining the narrow road on foot or in cars, mindless of the downpour which suddenly erupted. Many swore that this rain signaled a blessing for Red Bays and the Bahamas. The settlement's FNM supporters erupted in cheers as the returns came in declaring an overwhelming victory for their party; PLP supporters withdrew quietly into their homes. The FNM candidate for member of Parliament won handily in Red Bays and carried the majority in North Andros; Hubert Ingraham was again elected as prime minister. A convoy of cars and the school bus carried the revelers to the Deveaux headquarters, where they joined hundreds of others in celebration of a historic transition for Androsians; this marked the first time that the FNM had ever carried North Andros. The FNM's "Globalisation" policy, which promised a "Better, Better" life for Red Bays folks, delivered on some of the campaign promises; residents now have individual telephone service and a basketball court, and a few received government-supported part-time jobs. However, not all are satisfied as evidenced in these sentiments from a Red Bayan who wishes to remain anonymous: "Politicians make promises when dey runnin' for election, but when dey win, dey ain' check for you."

The Bahamas in the New Millennium

The Bahamas achieved its independence from Britain on July 10, 1973, but remains a British Commonwealth country. Approximately 65 percent of the country's population of 304,000 resides on New Providence, an eighty-square-mile island; the majority of people on this island reside in the capital city of Nassau. Nassau is the primary hub of tourism, the Bahamas' largest industry. Tourism generates an estimated 75 percent of the Bahamas' gross national product and employs two-thirds of the workforce, directly or indirectly. Social services in Nassau are heavily burdened by the combined effects of (1) the social, environmental, and economic costs associated with tourism; (2) substantial migration from the Family Islands; and (3) the large influx of Haitian refugees.[43]

Whether the Bahamas is governed by the FNM or the PLP, certain existential realities must be contemplated in strategic plans for the future: (1) the nation's geographic proximity to a superpower; (2) its scarce natural resources and resulting economic dependency; (3) its people's reluctance to rock the boat politically and in other ways (including confronting racial issues); and (4) its rapid modernization with the attendant social gains and losses.[44]

Traditionally, the Bahamas' economic strategies have emphasized the enclave, or vertical-integration mode of development, where the emphasis is on infrastructural facilities for the tourism industry, and where economic benefits accrue principally to transnational corporation stockholders.[45] Any benefits to the majority of Family Island communities, with the exceptions of Harbour Island and Grand Bahama Island, have been essentially fortuitous.

Revising this strategy to incorporate more integrated or horizontal developmental strategies that generate smaller-scale projects will be of particular benefit to Family Island communities like Red Bays. These types of projects will attract indigenous capital and management, essentially creating a redistribution of wealth and employment opportunities so scarce outside of Nassau. The FNM has affirmed new initiatives designed to exploit the tourism industry as a basis for horizontal developmental strategies that can potentially yield nationwide benefits. Linkages between the hospitality industry, agro-industries, fisheries, and light manufacturing may not only reduce imports but also increase the range and volume of exports.[46]

Ultimately, a critical confrontation may erupt on the issue of national self-determination and autonomy: a clash of domestic middle-class interests versus powerful international actors who control strategic resources.[47] Maingot comments that "theoretically, the only productive approach to understanding international relations is to assume that all national elites behave with what can be called strategic rationality, i.e. they will always attempt to maximize the benefits from any exchange. The elites of even the smallest state will take the choices and actions of others into account but they behave with as much self-interest as circumstances—and their opponents—permit."[48]

The marginalized black Bahamian must make herself or himself a visible force, enjoining the battle for her or his share of the country's wealth and for opportunities that are bound to emanate from the country's growing involvement in the global economy. The cultural and political well-being of the Bahamas largely depends upon Bahamians' bringing pressure upon politicians to keep their commitments and, importantly, engaging strategies of self-help. The Christian spirit which dominates the speech if not always the behavior of Bahamians—*aide toi et Dieu t'aidera* (God helps those who help themselves)—holds true.

In a country where the economy is dangerously skewed toward one industry—largely operative in only two cities—diversification is imperative. Reaching out to Family Island residents with strategies for their incorporation into plans for the new millennium, with business and life-sustaining opportunities that allow them and their children to live "down home" rather than be forced to migrate to Nassau for employment, is an essential ingredient for future prosperity in the Bahamas.

The FNM defines its "Globalisation" policy as an open invitation to foreign investment, what it considers the economic bridge to the new millennium. Elimination of the restrictive practices of Bahamianisation policies, including removal of political intervention in the issuance of business licenses, provides incentives for foreign investment. Through divestment of government-controlled industries, alliances can be formed between the government and the private sector.[49]

Most Caribbean economies are vulnerable, dependent upon external sources for the majority of their gross national product. Ripples that arise in source economies such as those of the United States and Great Britain can wreak tidal waves of economic destruction in the Caribbean. The impact of recent policy that restructures the lucrative offshore banking industry, their hand forced by the United States, will have a serious economic impact. When the U.S. embargo on Cuba is eventually lifted, this too has the potential to wield a major blow to the Bahamian economy's bottom line.

Well to me it is a gift . . . when I think back
on those, my ancestors, who had the courage to
leave Florida and come here . . . as I been told . . .
and settle in Red Bays. And went unnoticed for
so long. . . . These were very brave people to have
crossed the Gulf Stream and come over here in
Andros . . . to settle. I think that it is a rich
history. When I think back on the history
of Red Bays, I believe that I am a millionaire.

The Reverend Bertram A. Newton

5 ◎◎

De People Dem

Black Seminoles in the "Land behind God's Back"

The original 1821 Red Bays settlement was located three miles north of where
it is today. Devastating hurricanes forced evacuation of the original community
to Lewis Coppitt, which is at a higher elevation. Lewis Coppitt, named for the
Lewis family who purchased sixty-four acres of land there, was renamed Red
Bays around twenty years ago, as an instrument of social memory for the Black
Seminole descendants, and in the hope that this change would eliminate de-
rogatory references to the residents as "those people from de coppitt." The first
of the hurricanes that precipitated the evacuation of the original Red Bays
location occurred in 1866. Crown Commissioner Burnside surveyed the post-
hurricane damage and remarked: "I went to Red Bays and can scarcely picture
its destitution. Not a single house was left standing. Twenty-five houses were
destroyed and one-hundred-forty persons left homeless. . . . nine persons . . .
were drowned; five men and four children."[1]

In 1899 the community was once again ravaged by a hurricane. A Governor's
Office representative inspected the hurricane damage and reported that in Red

Bays he found: "this part of the Island for miles had been submerged. . . . parts of houses [were] made fast to the higher branches of the pine trees and numbers of vessels were scattered throughout the pine yard, in a more or less damaged condition. . . . I occupied myself in searching for any dead bodies that may have been in the vicinity as I had detected a most unpleasant odour. . . . My attention was called to a vessel which had been capsized and driven some distance into the pine yard. . . . there was a dead body on board."[2]

The loss of life was much greater this time, estimated at 100 to 150 persons.[3] The Bahamian government finally forced the community to abandon this site by threatening to refuse aid in the event of future hurricanes. The place to which many of them relocated was Lewis Coppitt. Others moved into adjacent areas in North Andros; "the Russells, the MacNeils and the Bowlegs moved to the eastern part of the island, to Lowe Sound, Nicoll's [sic] Town and Mastic Point."[4]

In 1937, anthropologist John Goggin was conducting an archaeological survey of Andros Island, and while there he visited the settlement of Mastic Point. There he met seventy-six-year-old Felix MacNeil, who declared that he was the grandson of Scipio Bowleg, a Seminole Indian (bush medicine) doctor who was among the first settlers of Red Bays. Goggin's journal entry reads as follows: "Tues., July 6 [1937] at Mastic Point, Andros Island: . . . Later went down to the water and sat under a big almond tree where a Negro named MacNeil was making a sculling oar. Spent the rest of the day there talking. MacNeil is from Red Bay and is part Indian."

MacNeil's family moved to Mastic Point after the 1866 hurricane devastated their home in the original Red Bays settlement. Goggin's encounters with MacNeil and others led him to conclude that he had "positively identified the legendary Indians of Andros Island as Seminole Negroes."[5] Felix MacNeil's great-grandson, Tellis Smith, related to me the oral history that he had learned from his grandmother Marion Pickstock, MacNeil's daughter. Tellis lives in Nassau but visits "down home" as frequently as possible where he maintains the family house. Tellis Smith learned the following from his grandmother:

> Well, my [maternal] grandmother was Marion Pickstock, and she told me about the Indian story and it goes like this: I understand they [the Seminoles] landed in Red Bay. Now the year I don't know. And they was the original Bowleg family.
>
> They migrated from Red Bay into Mastic Point. My mother was Aslea Pickstock and she marry into Smith. Pickstock was actually from England,

migrated to British Honduras, from British Honduras into Mastic Point. They [were Loyalist refugees who] came over on a boat called the *Potomac*. The *Potomac* got shipwrecked on Nassau bar. My granddaddy [who was a free man when he came from British Honduras] marry into Pickstock from the shipwreck and they stayed here [in Mastic Point] until his death.[6]

In 1980, shortly before her death, Smith's grandmother, Marion Pickstock, born in 1889, tape-recorded an interview that recalled her life and the unwritten history passed down from her father, Felix MacNeil. Her father was only five years old, and her mother just a baby, when the 1866 hurricane destroyed Red Bays. The 1899 hurricane was even worse; it destroyed boats, and "carried a lot of people off Andros' shore." Her house was swept away by the sea, forcing her family to move in with a neighbor in Mastic Point.[7] With the exception of two years spent working as a domestic in Florida, she lived her entire life on Andros Island.[8] Farming—including citrus orchards—fishing, and sponging were the primary means of subsistence for Androsians. She recalled that Lord Neville Chamberlain came to Mastic Point when she was two or three years old and stayed for about six years. He imported laborers from all over Andros, as well as from other islands, to work on his sisal plantation. The sisal plantation in Mastic Point, launched in the 1880s by Chamberlain, failed owing to the unsuitability of the soil and price competition.[9]

Prominent among Felix MacNeil's other descendants are his great-grandsons, brothers Percival MacNeil, M.D., and Lieutenant Commander Patrick MacNeil of the Bahamas Defence Force; both reside in Nassau.

The Wild Indians of Andros

Bahamians have had an enduring fascination with the legendary "wild Indians" of Andros Island, as affirmed in Mary Moseley's *Bahamas Handbook*: "It is to be hoped that the mystery of the interior of this island [Andros] will some day be unfathomed by means of aviation, when the allegations of explorers as to the existence of a tribe of people who hunt with bows and arrows can be investigated."[10]

A 1938 traveler's account in *Nassau Magazine* documented the isolated and subsistence-level lifestyle of the legendary Indians of Andros:

Ahead of us lay three diminutive dinghys, each with a small tattered sail, a baffling smell of sponge and dried fish, and a husky brown-skinned figure squatting amidship. How amazing to see these tiny boats so far from land, their owners apparently well satisfied in irking [*sic*] out a livelihood as "free-lance" spongers. Our guide told us that they came from a tribe that constantly move up and down the lonely shores of western Andros and are rarely seen even by the inhabitants of the established island settlements. For days on end the little dinghys stay at sea, finding their way by the colour of the water and the position of the stars.[11]

In a 1923 report, Andros wildlife warden E. W. Forsyth characterized the people of Red Bays and the nearby settlement of Lowe Sound as "nomads . . . who range the whole of this territory [and who had] a strain of Seminole blood."[12] They were a mysterious group, these Black Seminoles and their Baha-mian-born descendants, an enigma to most other Bahamians as well as Andros Island visitors. According to their oral history, that is just the way they wanted it. Red Bays remained an isolated community—accessible only by boat or foot-path through dense coppitts—until 1968, when a logging company cut a road through the bush in order to facilitate the removal of cut trees. This road led to the main (Queen's) highway that runs from the north to the central part of the island. Although the new twenty-mile road created some access into Red Bays, travel by automobile remained rather difficult because it was deeply rutted from the weather and was not paved until the late 1980s.

Red Bays was then, and yet remains, the only settlement on the western coast of Andros Island. The shoreline surrounding Red Bays has no sandy beach area, only mud. Andros Island, measuring 2,300 square miles, ranks as the largest island in the Bahamian archipelago and is alternately referred to as the "Big Yard" or the "Sleeping Giant," the former because of its vast area in comparison to other Bahamian islands, and the latter because of its untapped potential.[13] Comprising almost half of the longitudinal acreage of the entire island is a swampy, shallow area referred to as "the Mud." The Mud is the site of sponge beds that for many years were the foundation of the Bahamian economy and attracted Bahamians from many other islands seeking employment in the lu-crative trade. These fertile sponge beds proved lucrative primarily to Greek and white Bahamian merchants who implemented the "truck-and-credit" system, a system that exploited laborers. The truck-and-credit system was introduced in the Bahamas between 1811 and 1828 and operated such that "apprenticed liberated Africans were hired out by their masters for a specific salary but only received, in return for their labour, slave rations."[14] Employing this scheme, the merchant class effectively exploited both Africans and poor white Bahamians. This system closely resembled the "company store" scheme employed by southern U.S. plantation owners to exploit African-American sharecroppers: goods and supplies are advanced to workers, credited until a crop comes in. When the crop is sold, however, the worker more often than not ends up owing the "store" owner additional money, never realizing any profit. This cycle of debt continues ad infinitum.

Migration to Andros for sponging, once a major industry in the Bahamas, was especially great after Emancipation in 1834. This lucrative industry continued for over a century until 1938, when a mysterious bacterium or fungus attacked and destroyed the sponge beds, essentially wiping out the industry and decimating the Bahamian economy. Sponging eventually resumed but has never regained its economic dominance. After the demise of the sponging industry, Androsians began to make charcoal from the abundant trees of the pineyards, a profitable enterprise that was not subject to the truck-and-credit system; men were paid at point of sale. The sale of this product was more profitable to the people because they "got the money right in their hand; with sponging, [the] agent gave them money later. [They] only got share after expenses."[15]

Early Subsistence Strategies

In the early days, the men of Red Bays fished and hunted wild hogs, flamingoes, and other birds, trading these for flour, sugar, and tobacco from the spongers who migrated from other islands to work on the Mud.[16] Women were in charge of agriculture, growing corn, potatoes, pumpkins, and peas, and children of both genders worked the fields. They harvested the tubers, eddy, bay rush, and cassava, which the women grated and washed, a process required to, according to Rose Newton, "sweeten it and get the poison out." The resulting mash was then placed out in the sun to dry before pounding it into starch for flour.[17]

Corn, benny (sesame seed), pigeon peas, and beans were the main crops; these would often be shipped for eventual sale in Nassau. The profits were used to buy staple goods, which would later be distributed to members of the farmer's union association. This union, established by the Reverend Eldrack E. Newton (father of the Reverend B. A. Newton), was "a great help to the people and was bringing prosperity to the community until some evil-minded men got together and 'trusted' the goods and never paid, so that this discouraged the members, and the union was broken up."[18]

Eldrack Newton introduced fruit growing and hybridization to the farming program in 1945. He also established the All-Age School in Red Bays and became its first teacher. As a grant-in-aid teacher,

> He [E. E. Newton] was obligated to work for six months without payment. After that he was paid twelve pounds per year. He worked under these conditions for some time and later was able to have the designation of the school changed from "Grant-in-Aid" School to "Public" school by the kind permission of the late Rev. Daniel Dean, the writer's grandfather, he kept school in the Baptist Church for about four years. With the assistance of the community he was able to have built in 1939 a large school made of pine torch, wattles and tatch leaves. About 1941 a few bags of cement and a few pounds were given to make the floor. This building lasted for twenty one years before it collapsed.[19]

Eldrack Newton, a descendant of the original black Seminole settlers from Florida, was not originally from Red Bays; his family was among those who traveled further along the Andros eastern coast and arrived instead at Staniard Creek, a small settlement in Central Andros. Marriage brought him to Red Bays.

Bertram A. Newton has replaced his father as one of the most prominent men in Red Bays today. He is currently the pastor of New Salem Baptist Church (the only church in Red Bays), is a respected community leader and teacher, and was the principal of Red Bays Primary School for more than forty years before his retirement. He is also largely responsible for bringing attention to the existence of Black Seminole descendants in the Bahamas when, in 1968, he issued the first publication of their oral history—*A History of Red Bays, Andros, Bahamas*.

Contemporary Life

A large new sign along Queen's Highway marks the turn-off point for Red Bays, a unique Bahamian community. Approximately twenty miles down that side road—through dense coppitts filled with numerous varieties of pine trees and thatch plants—a small, wooden, hand-painted sign announces the entrance to the Red Bays settlement, pejoratively dubbed by some Bahamians as "the land behind God's back." Pictured on the sign is a fisherman, symbolizing the major subsistence activity of this community.

A 1969 visitor found Red Bays' eighty-eight residents "proud of their village and [their] past. . . . They build their roads with picks, hands, and tampers fashioned from wood. The children run barefoot through the winding dirt streets of the village. A transistor radio is their entertainment."[20] Much has changed in the settlement, as noted by Bertram Newton:

> The [first major] change was when our first school was built because before then, there was no school. We were teaching in the then Baptist church and after that then we went into the tatch tent that was use as schoolhouse. And so between the years 1957 and '60, I was then teaching outdoor on a flat floor. . . . the house was broken down from over the floor and [I] had my blackboard up in a tree. And so I held classes under that tree for five years. And so the change came when we had our first schoolhouse been built which I have entered in 1960 and that was a great change to us, and all the people of the community. Secondly, when we were building the school house, all the materials had to come round by water, by sea, in boats because we were isolated, geographically isolated and there were no way we could have [access] by land, other than by footpath. And so then in the year 1968 we had our first road . . . leading in from Lowe Sound, the nearest community [to] Red Bays. Before [the] road was completed I had bought my station wagon and had it reserved until then, then drove it down from the boat here. There seem to have been tremendous change [in Red Bays]. Along in those days we had to use wells, being dug by hand to get our water. Kerosene lamps and light woods that had to be used in the nighttime and we know nothing of search-lights when going for crabs because we had to go and get the light wood from the dry pine and use those to go for crab. Now we can take our searchlights and so forth and go get crab. We are able now to drive [into] Red Bay [from] the mail boat, all of our stuff can be driven in here. The first shop been here earlier . . . in the forties was Brother Lewis' father. They have had a shop, the first one ever been here, grocery shop, an then second to that was my shop which I kept two department. We had the dry good department and the grocery department. . . . [It] lasted for a few years and had to drop because of finance. We are able now to come in, bring whatever we want to. We have had machine, tractors, and so forth, coming in and rooting up the land whereby originally we had to use the machete or cutlass to cut the land. Today we can

just get a tractor that can do within about half an hour what we had to take about two, three months to do. A few people also are employed. Now employment has reached several people of Red Bays. Number one, we have got one of our own here as teacher—not prejudiced to say my wife—she's working. Then we've got a janitress employed here by the government. That seem to be great change. When compared to myself working more than fifteen years alone in a then grant-in-aid school before I was given a second teacher. Well I have done all my teaching with that one teacher for forty-one and a half years. Now I'm retired and staying with the church. And another change is that we have had a wooden church building, now we've got a stone church building that can be match with any other small building in other communities. We can worship as we will, without interfering, without having to move in the rain. We are able to worship God without interference. Another one is the water coming in here, sharing with no other community. Then we've got our lights. You know it look pretty fair in the night when you are coming into the community and looking after the lights. Then it tells you that there is somebody alive here in Red Bays. The lights came after the road. It was sometime when the first minister [of Parliament] to work came here, the Honorable Darrell Rolle, the representative for this area. He felt that Red Bays should not be isolated from the other communities and he had seen to it that we had just what was in the other communities.

The dirt road into Red Bays, carved out of the pineyard in 1968 with attendant ceremony, was finally "tarred" in the late 1980s, allowing all of the children of Red Bays to attend North Andros High School in Nicholls Town.[21] Before the road was paved, only children who went to live with relatives in other Andros settlements, such as Lowe Sound, Mastic Point, or Nicholls Town, attended high school. An unfortunate reality for these Red Bays children, who are predominantly from poor families, is that they are often subjected to harsh ridicule from other students; they are called "wild hogs," a reference likening them to the feral pigs that roam the bush in Andros.

My first impression of the community in 1996 revealed a harmonious scenario: where children from other families are handed a plate of food if they happen to be in a neighbor's home at meal time; where food, clothes, tools, brooms, and other items are readily borrowed; where doors are left unlocked. This "rose-colored glasses" fog, one that most ethnographers experience, cleared after a while, when the underlying problems that plague most small communities came to light. Various animosities that divide the community into factions made it difficult for this ethnographer to remain neutral, especially because I lived in a family home.

One of the major activities in the community is gossip. Since, as most residents will tell you, there is absolutely nothing to do in "boring" Red Bays, people delve into one another's personal lives and conjure up details to spice things up if need be. Gossip sessions were common at the BATELCO (Bahamas Telephone Corporation) building, which served as a community gathering place. Until December 1998 the settlement's only telephone access was at this building. People would gather there daily, "hailing" anyone in earshot (which might be a few houses away) who had a telephone call, or the operators would take a message for calls to be returned later. BATELCO was practically the only source of employment within the community itself. A few other Red Bays residents had government jobs there: schoolteacher (Rose Newton, wife of the Reverend B. A. Newton); school janitress; school lunch preparer (for especially needy children eligible for the government's school lunch program); trash collector (a rotating appointment); high school bus driver; and road caretakers who operated the "bush hog" or weed trimmer during holiday seasons. When the BATELCO office closed in 1998, residents had their own private telephones installed, thus eliminating an important gathering place for the community. It also eliminated much of the substance for gossip sessions because nosy residents could no longer tune into certain radio and television stations to intercept personal conversations as they had from the wireless BATELCO service.

Several residents operate small "shops" where dry and canned goods, sodas, bread, and other food and sundry items can be purchased. These shops are generally not well stocked, and for fresh vegetables one must travel the twenty-mile route out of the settlement to reach the next-closest store along Queen's Highway. For many years, one of the shop owners in Red Bays also controlled the only gas pump in the settlement. Twenty miles outside the main road, she wielded a lot of control over the movements of people who don't often keep their tanks on "full." In 2000, a second gas pump was added, owned and operated by another resident. Despite this, access to gasoline in the settlement— necessary for boats as well as cars—is still not reliable. In addition to supply problems, politics and personal relations can often determine whether you can fill up or not.

Incredibly diverse and seemingly contradictory aspects of existence are extant in this settlement. Just twenty years ago, the majority of residents lived in wood frame houses with thatched roofs,[22] cooked outdoors on open fires or in detached structures built for use as kitchens (a strategy still utilized when the dry gas tanks run out), and had no telephone service, no indoor plumbing, and few cars. Major transitions occurred in the settlement as a result of an economic boom from the 1960s to 1980s, a boom that is attributed to several factors. First, logging companies, hired to harvest the vast local pineyards, provided employment for some men in the community. Second, removal of the logs required the construction of a twenty-mile stretch of road; this new road facilitated unprecedented access into Red Bays by vehicle rather than solely by footpath or boat, as had been the case for almost 150 years. This development enhanced the subsistence economy by providing residents with cash from new customers for their produce, seafood, and baskets. Third, profits from the lucrative drug trade, rampant in the Bahamas during the 1980s, filtered into the community. These events dramatically transformed lifestyles in the settlement for many, but not all, residents. There is a segment of the community who, whether by conscious choice or lack of networks, did not share in the economic boom. Although cement-block or board (frame) houses, complete with ceramic tile floors and satellite dishes in the yards, have replaced the majority of the austere housing, a few houses still lack indoor kitchens, plumbing, and electricity.

Kinship and Social Structure

Definitions of household composition and social structure in the Caribbean vary significantly according to author and agenda, and have been the subject of much debate.[23] Eurocentric models of kinship often distort what consultants tell anthropologists about the nature of their household and social structure. These distortions occur because conceptualizations of kinship are not merely functional, but contextual and, therefore, should not be interpreted via a Eurocentric paradigm. Our concern must be redirected to focus on the emic perspective, the conceptual system that reveals what their cultural practices mean to the people themselves.[24] The interposition of nonnative referential terms derived from Eurocentric ideas of kinship classifications that dichotomize kin into consanguines (blood relatives) and affinals (in-laws), and define the nuclear family structure as the norm, consigns most Caribbean, as well as many other so-called Third World societies to the realm of "bizarre, irrational, and difficult to appreciate."[25] In the Caribbean, kinship ties are culturally, rather than biologically, defined. From the earliest days of their arrival, Africans enslaved in the Americas extended the bonds of kinship beyond the boundaries of individual households, a practice consistent with the cultural traditions of their African origins and reinforced by the conditions of their enslavement. They addressed one another as brothers and sisters, uncles and aunts, and so on, conferring the status of kin on men and women who were unrelated by blood or marriage.[26] The theoretical models of Smith (1988) and Gonzalez (1984) are particularly useful in the analysis of Red Bays' households and reflect the extended kinship parameters mentioned above. Smith characterizes the West Indian family as a "domestic system, which does not confine relations within an easily defined or bounded household."[27] Gonzalez defines Garifuna households as "ephemeral transitory agglomerations of kin who cluster together when their personal needs compel them to seek succor and subsistence, or when they can be drawn in (even coerced) to help support others."[28] Both of these models are useful because the composition of Red Bays' households sometimes changes daily, as "relatives" decide to reside in Red Bays' households for brief or extended periods of time for various reasons. In Red Bays the term "relative" includes consanguineal, affinal, and fictive kin; residence is more definitive than biology in their kinship relations.

The Red Bays definition of "relative" also includes "adopted" family members. Adoptions occur under various circumstances, including abandonment, orphanage, or "giving" a child to relatives or a childless couple to raise as their own. In most cases these "adoptions" are not transacted legally, but nonetheless are considered binding commitments. People are also designated as "goddy," or godparent, and that role holds a considerable responsibility toward a child's well-being.

Relatives also include sisters and brothers who are "outside" children. Outside children are those a man fathers with women other than his legal wife, a widespread phenomenon in Red Bays as well as other parts of the Bahamas. In many instances, the children who are born from the legal union often consider these outside children full siblings. For example, one woman's father claimed a total of thirty-eight children with five women, including her mother, his only legal wife. The result is that she has many siblings at or near her same age. She (and her mother) always knew about her father's outside liaisons. She regards most of these other women warmly—some as "play" or surrogate mothers—

and their children as brothers and sisters, making no distinctions of "half-" or "step-." Another woman relates a similar perspective:

> My mummy and daddy have fourteen children. He [her father] have eight outside children, six with [one woman] and two with [another woman]. Six of them [outside children] live right here in Red Bay. With me, right, I don't take them as no different, I accept them as my blood brothers and sisters. One time when we was younger growing up we used to have problems. You know, because like during daddy with his sweetheart, mummy would go calling him and they would start ravving. And after we get grown up and get out of it, we [she, her siblings and the outside children] associate good. Mummy she got to where she accept it.

Because of the tendency of men to father children with multiple women, "consanguineal relatives through the father appear more numerous than those through the mother."[29] Historically, women may have disapproved of the extra-marital relationships, but realistic opportunities to leave a "cheating" spouse were nonexistent and things have not changed much to this day.

Demographics and Household Composition

There were forty-four households and a population of 283 in Red Bays (as of 1998), and children constitute 81 percent of the population. Most households consist of three or four generations, with various combinations of adult siblings and their children, grandparents, nephews and nieces, grandchildren, great-grandchildren, godchildren, and adopted children. The emphasis is on the mother-child bond, not the conjugal unit.[30] This type of family structure permits "instability in conjugal ties, while maintaining great stability in both the family and kinship systems."[31]

One of the classification systems, or taxonomies, commonly used by Caribbean scholars describes three forms of "marriage": legal marriage; common law (conjugal or residential) unions; and visiting (extra-residential) unions. Employing these categories, the data from the British Caribbean reveal that 48 percent of all households consist of legally married unions, and about 20 per cent are of the conjugal/residential type.[32] The trend varies regionally, depending upon ethnicity, class, and historical factors. The Red Bays community varies significantly from these legal marriage statistics. Fifty percent of Red Bays' forty-four households are couple-headed. In 77 percent of these, the man and woman have been legally married. Twenty percent are single-female-headed households. Thirty percent of Red Bays' households are single occupant households, all of which are composed of men who are transitory residents, dividing their residency between Red Bays, other Family Islands, and, in particular, Nassau, owing to the pervasive lack of employment opportunities in the Family Islands. Consequently, Nassau is becoming overpopulated, suffering all the concomitant social problems that this invites, while the Family Islands' populations continue to decline.

The majority of men currently have or have in the past had extraresidential unions with "sweethearts"[33] who are "down de road" (that is, in Red Bays) or "up de shore" (in other communities of Andros), from which liaisons outside children are born. The research of Caribbeanist R. T. Smith revealed that "masculinity is not defined in terms of a man's occupation nor whether he has a job at all. Instead, it is defined by his number of sexual conquests or by 'having children all about.'"[34] The traditional origin of polygynous relationships, common in Red Bays and in the Bahamas in general, can be variously attributed. These multipartner relationships were features of many African and indigenous cultures and were "actively promoted by the European slave-owners who encouraged, even compelled, the breeding of many children to increase the labor force."[35] Regardless of where the tradition originates, men do a considerable amount of "eye shopping."

The majority of Red Bays' women have borne children from multiple unions. Most have had at least one child before legally marrying, yet no distinctions are expressed concerning the biological status of each child within the household, such as half- or stepsister or stepbrother. This pattern of relationships between biologically and nonbiologically related household members is corroborated by previous research conducted in a South Andros community, where Keith Otterbein determined that "membership in a corporate group rather than consanguineal bonds creates relationships."[36]

Often women will attest to male headship of their households even though they themselves actually function as leaders in household decision-making and income-producing activities. These claims may result from what Helen I. Safa terms the "ideological norm of male dominance."[37] Joycelin Massiah concurs, stating that "identifying the head of a household is always problematic, since it involves both an objective and a subjective element. Usually men as 'breadwinners' are assumed to be heads of households. This is not always the case. However, culture and patriarchy have so institutionalized male headship that quite often reported proportions may be over-rated."[38] Although most of the men have no steady "breadwinner" capacity in Red Bays and often subsist day to day by fishing, many (but not all) women seek to associate themselves with a particular man who controls her activities to a greater or lesser extent. In his study of household structure in South Andros, Otterbein reports that even in situations where the woman is the property owner, "the man is director of the household,"[39] and therefore, it is classified as male-headed.

In Red Bays, only one man is employed in wage labor outside the settlement. All of the others engage in fishing, sponging, and woodcarving, weather permitting. Many own fifteen-foot Boston whaler boats, equipped with outboard motors, that are their primary means of livelihood. The size of these boats, however, prohibits travel on the sea unless there is minimal wind. On the frequent occasions when the wind is too high, many men spend the day working on boats and vehicles, or consuming intoxicants, rum and otherwise.

The money earned from selling sponges, fish, and crabs is often spent buying "drinks all around," all night long until the funds are depleted—often before his mate or children have received any of the money. This happens because one of the sponge merchants often sets up a bar after paying the men, where their profits conveniently boomerang back to the merchant in the form of alcohol sales. Most women grumble among one another, but don't often confront the men, stating simply, "No diffren, mon. He still de boss." Male dominance is sometimes contested, most often by withholding sexual relations.

Power relationships that existed in colonial times and persist today have critical implications for the formation and analysis of kinship structures in the Caribbean. Taxonomies of household structure and kinship in the Caribbean measured against the dominant Eurocentric model of the nuclear family uphold power, and "power maintains the order of the world."[40] By employing these categories that correspond to a specific conceptual order of reality, we suppress, delegitimize, or negate subaltern epistemologies. Contemporary anthropologists must confront the institutional gatekeepers who perpetuate "universal" definitions of "normal" social organization. Implementing new strategies and methods of analysis grounded in non-Eurocentric models is a useful approach to this task.[41]

The Culture of Gender and Sexuality

Gender is a dynamic and dialectical cultural system; it "interacts with and affects social structures and culture and is also affected by the same."[42] Red Bays mirrors the construction of gender roles in the broader Bahamian society. Patriarchal social organization, predicated upon male dominance over the activities—productive and reproductive—of women, defines the community culture. In the Bahamas, as in other parts of the British Caribbean or West Indies region, women have always worked outside the home in large numbers, and as a result, there is no strict private/public dichotomy. Gender asymmetry, however, is reinforced by an androcentric political system; women did not win suffrage in the Bahamas until 1962. When the black-Bahamian-led Progressive Liberal Party (PLP) wrenched political control from the Bay Street Boys in 1967, the status of women in the Bahamas remained largely unchanged. At a 1997 Free National Movement (FNM) campaign rally in North Andros Island, Prime Minister Hubert Ingraham shed light on the PLP's lack of initiative in this arena when he announced that: "For twenty years in the Bahamas the PLP could not find a single person with a gown-tail who they felt was worthy to sit around the cabinet table of the Bahamas. For twenty years, no female could be a minister in their government. And today, they have 17 seats in the House [of Assembly]—it ain't for long—and not a single woman. And they ain't running a single woman for a single seat in this election."[43]

As is the case with many political speeches, the prime minister took some license with the facts. The PLP actually had placed several women into candidacy during their tenure: Ruby Ann Darling, who was elected for part of the Exuma Islands, and several others who were unsuccessful in their bids for seats, including Pleasant Bridgewater, Michelle Pindling, Sheila Glinton, and Mispah Tertullien. Among the significant sociocultural changes brought about by the FNM when it gained control in 1992 was the inclusion of women in high-level government positions. Women served as members of Parliament, senators, and as heads of several Bahamian government ministries in the FNM government.

Caribbeanist, Helen Safa, suggests that "adult status and feminine identity among Caribbean women are based on motherhood and not marriage, and most low-income women start to have children long before they marry, often in their teens."[44] The above-mentioned standards apply in Red Bays, where many women do not complete high school because they get pregnant at a young age, and men display obvious pride in these pregnancies that represent the manifestation of their sexual prowess. The Reverend Bertram Newton, religious leader and pastor of Red Bays' only church, expressed these views on community attitudes about pregnancies among unmarried women and the phenomenon of "outside" children:

> The church in our Baptist society, we do not scorn the person. Because consider yourself to be in the same predicament; that can happen to anyone. It's an uncertain thing that you can't control. You can control it in a sense. But the person, the child don't know how to control it. You may tell them but they will not heed what you say. And if they do not know and they get themself into trouble you just can't throw them away. You got to let them know that they are still loved, you know, and ask them not to make the same mistake. That's all you can do. But I would not just fuss them out, because I remember the story of those who drag a woman to Jesus and said "Sir, this woman was caught in adultery, at the very act, what you have to say about that?" Moses say, "Take them and stone them." Jesus say, "You who don't have a sin cast the first stone on her."[45]

Although the community overtly disapproves of premarital sex and pregnancies among unwed mothers, the mother (unless very young) and her child are not ostracized. Rather, children are viewed as a "blessing," regardless of the circumstances of birth. Research in Jamaica concurs with this, finding that "sexuality is usually conceptually linked with the desire to create children. For both men and women, perceptions of self-identity and social power are contingent upon the expression of sexual potency, which is confirmed by the birth of children."[46]

This phenomenon may also be partially attributed to the legacy of enslavement, when (albeit under coercive circumstances) some dubious "status" possibly accrued. According to the U.S. Federal Writers' Project:

> The rapid breeding of more slaves—to replace deaths and natural retirements in some cases and for purposes of sale and trade in others—was desirable to most plantations. Thus we find several of them had women whose sole task was to serve as "breeders." These breeders had only one job, childbearing. On some plantations they did little else, except occasional

light work around the house of the master. They would be mated with the most promising-looking of the men, repeatedly. It was not unusual for a woman to bear twelve or fourteen children during her active career as a "breeder."[47]

As a consequence of limited economic and social opportunities for men and women in many postcolonial Caribbean societies, procreation is viewed as a means of gaining status.[48] Paradoxically, there is still a double standard that recognizes the natural proclivity (even duty) of males to express their sexuality by their late teens, while women are more valued as marriage partners if they have retained their virginity.[49]

Contemporary Subsistence Strategies

Contemporary livelihood activities in Red Bays differ considerably from those of the original settlers who grew, caught, or raised everything they ate. When the Black Seminoles were "discovered" by the customs officer in 1828, they were subsisting in peace, farming and fishing to adequately meet their needs. Red Bays' men harvested the rich sponge beds of the Mud and were joined by Bahamians from various other islands seeking employment. Some of these men had unions, conjugal or legal, with Red Bays' women. Other men labored on the Chamberlain sisal plantation, located in Mastic Point, where an 1894 *Report on Visit to Andros Fibre Plantation of Mr. Chamberlain* noted that there were "5,000 acres being cultivated at that time in an area that had been essentially wilderness four years prior"; "people earn their money before spending it: no truck and credit system. Mr. Chamberlain testifies to the steady industry of the labourers and general good conduct . . . no rum shop in the neighbourhood."[50]

In the 1940s, Red Bays men found alternative sources of income by going to work in the United States on the "contract," essentially becoming migrant farm workers. One of these men was William "Old Iron" Colebrooke, who relates in an interview that "When I was much younger I used to go on the contract in Florida and pick sour, harvesting cane, harvesting corn, orange, watermelon, cucumber, celery, and apple."

Today, the economic foundation of Red Bays continues to be built upon fishing, crabbing, sponging, basketry, and woodcarving—subsistence activities that are predominantly gender specific. Men do the fishing; women infrequently accompany them, although they never drive the boats. Fishing, or "fishnin," as many pronounce it, varies seasonally because there are regulations governing the harvesting of particular species, such as crawfish. The primary catch is snapper, red or gray. A few men in the settlement, however, have gained excellent reputations for their skill at bonefishing. Tourists, longing for a real challenge in fishing, come from around the world to participate in this "sport." Most often, however, fishing is a family (male members primarily) or small-group activity, for subsistence or profit. Occasionally, a large group of men go out to sea for the catch. When they return successful, they might have hundreds of fish; they set up an assembly line process of scaling, gutting, washing, and packing the fish for sale, either to a buyer or taking it by boat to Nassau, where they can make a greater profit. Generally fishing excursions are one-day trips that begin at daybreak. During crawfish season, however, these trips may last longer, since they have to retrieve their traps from distant waters. Because most of them own only small fifteen-foot fishing boats that cannot withstand high seas, men are often prevented from going out when there is more than a hint of breeze on shore. This generally means that their families will not have much to eat. Occasionally the men hunt wild boar and birds. Flamingoes were once widely caught and eaten, but this activity is now illegal because of overhunting.

Crabbing is a seasonally lucrative subsistence strategy. At night during the rainy season, the crabs abandon their flooded homes—which are burrows in the soil—and go walking. They are then hunted by men, women, and children wielding flashlights or torches to light their paths. Once caught, the crabs are placed in crab pens, where they are fed with various concoctions, most including some rice, so that they will fatten up and command a higher market price. Crabs are often sold to middlemen, outside merchants who drive into the settlement knowing that Red Bays' crab pens are usually well stocked. These crabs can sell for up to four dollars each in the Nassau marketplace. Crab and dough and crab and rice are the savored cuisine of this season throughout the Bahamas.

Sponging activities lie solely within the masculine realm. Goggin's 1937 journal described Felix MacNeil's sponging activity: "MacNeil's sponge boat came in today. It will leave soon for a two week voyage to the Mud. Each man will take 2 lbs. of lard, 6 lbs. rice, 4 lbs. sugar, and 25 lbs. of flour for his ration for that length of time."[51]

Before 1938, when the sponge beds were extremely fertile, Red Bays men would be gone for several weeks, returning only for water and wood for galley cooking. The sponge beds have revitalized since the devastating bacterium outbreak, but sponging is no longer a major source of income. Several men are woodcarvers rather than seamen, and a few women are also learning this craft.

Currently there is no substantial farming activity in Red Bays; some people cultivate small subsistence gardens, using the cutlass as their primary tool. The majority, however, are almost entirely reliant upon store-bought goods, fruit trees, and the sea for their survival.

The oral history reveals quite a different scenario of life in Red Bays when today's adults were children. Most of the community—men, women, and children—boarded a sailing ship every January for the trip to Billy Coppitt, located south of Red Bays, where they would spend six months farming. There was no strict division of labor; everyone farmed the fields. Omelia Marshall was in charge of both work duties and school lessons there. These lessons consisted of reading from the only book available—the Bible. This accounts for the fact that many adults in the settlement, who are otherwise semiliterate or illiterate, are adept at quoting Bible verses memorized over those years. The farming tradition is clearly among the least desirable of livelihood strategies for the younger generations of Red Bayans,[52] despite Andros Island's vast potential for farming. Unfortunately, this negative attitude about farming is one shared by other Bahamians, as illustrated in these comments: "I'll do farming and fishing, but not on such a scale as to really make money because I proud and farming is for Haitians."[53]

Traditionally, land is primarily designated as "generation property"; it is jointly held by family members and cannot be sold. Generation property is designated as such when a man leaves a will naming his male and female descendants, generation after generation, as his heirs and his eldest son as the executor, who can then appoint his successor.[54]

Basket Sewing—Straw Work

Central to the community fabric of the Red Bays settlement is the extended family of Omelia Marshall, eighty-year-old widowed matriarch of Red Bays. She boasts of being the originator of the unique basketry crafted in Red Bays. Taught by her father, who at first sewed the baskets with sea grass, Mrs. Marshall introduced innovations in styles and materials; she uses various types of "top" from palm thatch plants in place of the original sea grass.

Journal Entry 2/18/97

Mrs. Marshall's father (Scipio Demeritte) used a needle he made from light wood to sew baskets. She now uses a metal needle, supplied by "the white people." Her father cut fanner grass (sea grass) on the edge of the sea and made baskets from this. He could only make the fanner, but she started making them with covers (lids). Then she and others started improvising more designs. She started in the 1980s making baskets with "top" instead of sea grass and sold the first one to a white man, "Mr. Steve," who was working on the road. (The main road into Red Bays just got "black-topped" or paved in the late 1980s.) She tells me, "I didn't ask nothing! I gone!" (i.e. she didn't need anyone's permission to make this change, she just went ahead and did it!). She says that people in the settlement laughed at her, saying "What Momma think she doing? That boat will never float!" But when they saw her making lots of money from her new style baskets, they stopped laughing and started making these baskets too. She told them emphatically, "The boat floatin'!" (See figs. 2, 10, 11.)

Marshall Town, as she calls her compound, consists of five various-size frame dwellings built in an irregular circle, a Seminole-style chickee structure called a "tatch camp," and a hand drawn well, its opening covered with a thin board. There is no electricity, which Mrs. Marshall regards as "dangerous." Mrs. Marshall and three generations of her family—grandchildren, great-grandchildren, and great-great-grandchildren (biological and adopted)—live amongst precarious rock outcroppings and dense vegetation that includes cassava, eddy, and corn, as well as coconut, sapodilla, apple, and pear trees. Her children, three daughters and two sons, still also live in Red Bays, though not in Marshall Town. At dawn, or when "day clean," as she says, she can be found cultivating her garden with cutlass in hand and, later, seated on a broken chair or crate, joining her family, who sew baskets throughout the day under a canopy of coconut palm and fruit trees. The Marshall Town "compound" is similar to the "yard" system in Jamaica,[55] and to that of their distant "relatives" from the Sea Islands of South Carolina, another place where Africans were isolated for a very long time. Mary A. Twining and Keith E. Baird found a remarkably similar residence pattern while conducting their research on Sea Island culture:

Among traditional African Americans in South Carolina, there are domiciliary complexes or "compounds" consisting of several households assembled on the basis of kinship and economic constraints. Organized around the oldest progenitor couple, often around the senior surviving female progenitor—since women tend generally to outlive men—such a complex of households encompasses brothers and sisters and their families all living in houses close by. This residence pattern closely approximates its African counterparts.... Members of the family sit in groups under the trees making baskets, joking, and generally enjoying one another's company.[56]

Mrs. Omelia Marshall came to Red Bays at age nine from Lowe Sound, another of the settlements to which Black Seminole refugees fled after the hurricanes devastated the original Red Bays site. At age sixteen, she was taught by her grandmother, Martha Celeste Russell—sister of John Russell who is listed on the 1828 customs' roster—to plait thatch, and her "auntie-in-law" showed her how to sew baskets, which she learned so well that she "beat her at it."[57] Her aunt and father would sew with the sea grass, fashioning wide fanner baskets used to clean husks from grits, and benny (sesame).

A major source of income in the settlement, especially for women, is from the sale of baskets. Although it is mostly women who sew baskets, some of the most skilled workers are men. The few men whom I observed sewing baskets are perceived by others in the settlement as persons who are either too weak to go out to sea, or who do not own or have access to a boat. The income from baskets is neither regular nor dependable. Most people sew baskets with hopes of selling them to tourists, who come into Red Bays only infrequently: expatriate villa residents from Nicholls Town, United States students from Forfar Field Station, and workers (typically U.S. citizens also) from AUTEC naval base, both located in Central Andros. Some women consign their baskets to another woman, who makes several trips each week outside of the settlement to sell these to tourists at the few fishing and diving resorts of Andros Island. Baskets are also shipped to Nassau, where they command a premium price in tourist shops; the original purchase prices receive a considerable markup. Red Bays' baskets have gained a reputation for their distinctive and sturdy construction and uniquely attractive styles, which can be singled out immediately because they are unlike any other baskets crafted in the Bahamas. A website advertising these baskets is a "work-in-progress" that will, hopefully, provide new economic opportunities in this community. In 1992 members of the Red Bays community were invited to Washington, D.C., to participate in a celebration of Caribbean culture sponsored by the Smithsonian Institution. There they demonstrated thatching techniques, basketry, and woodcarving in a celebration of Bahamian culture.

Status in Red Bays is based upon consumerism; he or she who has the most money, the latest Nike sneakers, the better house or better "trans"—Bahamian slang for a car or other vehicle—also has the most clout. There is a curious mixture of capitalism in Red Bays. It can be characterized as early industrial capitalism[58] because of their isolation and the lack of wage-labor opportunities. Many people emigrate off-island, seeking employment primarily in Nassau or Freeport, the tourist meccas. The Reverend Benjamin Lewis, assistant pastor of the New Salem Baptist Church, laments how large the Red Bays community might be today had better employment opportunities been available there: "There's no job, no nothing for the people them here. But I look forward that one day God will open up a way that there will be job flowing through. I may not be here, cause I know my course has almost done come, but I look forward that this coming generation, that they will have a better success, not only Red Bays, but through North Andros and the Bahamas as a whole."

Remittances and child-support payments are not much of an economic factor in Red Bays. The nominal income from these sources, as well as government welfare subsidies, does, however, play a role in the local economy.

Mrs. Marshall complains bitterly about young people in the settlement "tiefing" (stealing) from her small garden and fruit trees.[59] She explains that it was not that way in the old days; people worked hard for their daily subsistence:

When the day clean, we go this way to Robert Coppitt to dig wild yam and catch crab. We cut cabbage and bring this. . . . You can't have no kerosene [in those days]; you bring light wood. Then catch fire in the camp. In the days gone by when you come from crab, you go catch fire and cook your little wild yam and your little crab. Tomorrow, when the day clean, you're gone again! Sometimes you go way down the shore in them deep creeks and them deep water to get bay rush. You stop at Cedar Coppitt to catch crab, you catch soldier [crab]. When you done grater this [she's holding up a bay rush plant] and wash this and settle this over, you done wash this in water twice, you may go and mix this bread and roll it up. Then you boil the crab and you get this bay rush bread and get the flour bread it's better.[60]

The bay rush she speaks of is a poisonous tuber that has to be prepared carefully to make it edible.

When you done wash this bay rush, you supposed to settle it over in a tub of water. Then after that done settle over, you take the big spoon and you take out all the brown starch off the top. Then you take the big spoon and dig out the big ole hunks of white starch and you put it in the flour bag to drain. When it done drain then you go and you make your gola. Your gola is two-piece of starch and a little bit of salt, make your gola. And put your starch in the tray and mix your bread with the gola and bake your bread. When you done bake your bread you boil the crab, and that's bay rush bread and crab! [Bay rush], that make all kind of bread. What?! That make all kind of cake. God planted that bay rush.

She learned this technique from the old Seminoles, as she calls her ancestors. She cannot eat the bay rush bread, however, because it caused her to contract typhoid fever and, consequently, she says, caused her hearing loss.

Going into the pineyard was not without its hazards as she explains: "You had one woman gone down in one of the pineyards, and when she got down in there the yerhoo [a creature of Andros folklore] was coming and they got keep on catching fire to keep off the yerhoo, until the day clean. After the day clean, they jump in the water and leave from there, down where they lay coontie root. Study well coontie root." Seminoles and Black Seminoles in Florida used coontie to make sofkee.

Children were also adept at bush survival techniques. Old Iron Colebrooke describes how he would spend months on end in the bush, or "wilderness," as he terms it, where he escaped from his physically abusive father. He would leave by moonlight, having packed his provisions earlier and stashed them on the roadside to be retrieved on his way out of the settlement. His invaluable tools were

one cutlass and something like a ting-um you could burn lint. Take some cloth and bundle a bunch of cloth up together and when you done bundle it up together, you take it in your pocket. And something like a cow horn and you pack it in the cow horn. And it will stay in that cow horn as long as you want it and it can't wet. You don't have no match. Take a piece of small iron and you hit it on the side of the cutlass. The more you hit it on the cutlass you see a spark of fire drop from the cutlass. And you hit it and hit it then when you see it start smoking then you take out that piece o' grass and you rub that grass up and hold that to the wind. And when that catch, you put it down on the ground and you broke up a little wood on top o' that and you get your fire. [With the cutlass] I could cut pine to build just enough little camp for me to stretch out in the wilderness. And if I go in the back here not so far from the settlement, three, four miles back in the woods, I be there for months and months. I pull cabbage, dig wild yam and roast them 'til I go out on the bay at Cedar Coppitt and if I meet anybody camp on the bay and they have grater, [and] crocus bag [to put crabs in], flour bag more than one. Or take a sheet, find tin and carry [borrow] it. And I carry a bucket, bring it back inside the camp. [He would use items then return them.] I dig my well. I dig my bay rush, I grater it. I build a troho and I full it up with chaff and I let it stay in there until it sour. And when it sour I take the fresh chaff and wash the stale chaff. But I never wash it until the young moon to the wester. Catch crab, carry starch, and sell starch by the quart [for 50 cents' worth] they give you a dollar. Until I get enough to buy me a half sack of flour and a package of rice and a couple cans of sweeten milk and fat like lard and whatnot. And I pack that up in one bag and I throw that up on my shoulder and I gone.[61]

Religion

As is the case in most of the Bahamas, religion plays a central role in everyday speech and in politics. Bible verses easily roll off the tongues of even intoxicated men. Their Black Seminole ancestors who came to Red Bays, according to the Reverend Bertram Newton, were already Christians. Exposure to various Christian religions was commonplace on North American plantations; these teachings were often used to pacify the enslaved. In particular, slaveowners and their hired preachers favored the Book of Paul and used his pronouncement to "obey your master" as a control agent.

New Salem Baptist Church is the only church building in Red Bays. The congregation has dwindled to a faithful few on most Sundays, far different than in the past, according to Bertram Newton. Because of a shortage of clergy on Andros Island, Newton is also pastor, once a month, at the Zion Baptist Church in Staniard Creek, a settlement located on the eastern coast of Central Andros, approximately forty miles from Red Bays. The congregation of this church has few, predominantly elderly, members. His position as visiting pastor at Zion Baptist Church affords him an opportunity to visit with his relatives in Staniard Creek—where his grandfather Moses Newton originally settled in the 1820s— and he typically joins them for dinner after church. There are also a few adherents to the Seventh Day Adventist denomination living in Red Bays, but they worship in their homes; occasionally a pastor visits to perform services for them. While conducting my research, I attended services of both these denominations. Many people were surprised that I was in attendance, often singling me out for (unwanted) recognition; never had an "American woman" lived among them and, in some ways, become a part of the community fabric.

In addition to Baptist and Seventh Day Adventist, there are numerous other denominations represented on Andros Island: Mennonite, Methodist, Baptist, Anglican, Jehovah's Witnesses, and Church of God.

Folklore

When archaeologist John Goggin visited Andros Island in 1937, he wrote journal entries that shed some light on the preoccupations of Androsians he met. Goggin remarked that "probably religion and spirits are the main things that the Negroes talk about." Stories of spirits and ghosts abound in Red Bays. There are certain areas of the pineyard (or coppitt) where these are known to dwell. Some of the children pointed out to me, but would not venture into, several areas reputedly "haunted" by headless horses and other frightening phantoms.

Mary Moseley cites Andros Island as "the only island in the Bahamas that has a native folklore, the others having adopted the African, and quaint stories are told by old residents of the chickannies [otherwise spelled chickcharnies]."[62]

According to legend, the chickcharnies,

> in making their nests, tied branches across the pathways past which the cruel slavemasters dared not go for fear they would never return. Some people say that "Chickcharnie" was the name of a tribe of Indians who used to help the slaves, but this has never been proved. On the other hand it is quite definitely known that these little bird-like creatures helped them. Like the Leprechauns they have many human attributes but they also have terrific power. They can pass over great distances, they can go through walls. They cast no shadow because they are known to be in touch with man's higher nature.[63]

I asked Daisy Jumper, who is a self-described "full blood, Red Stick Seminole" and who accompanied me on a visit to Red Bays, whether she has ever heard the word "chickcharnie" in the Miccosukee or Creek languages that she speaks. Daisy is recognized for her knowledge of Seminole history and culture.[64]

She can think of no similar word in her language, nor similar folklore about this owl-like creature, although the owl is an important symbolic feature in the Seminole culture.

Other fabled creatures specific to Andros folklore include the evil Lusca, a half-dragon, half-octopus creature that lives in caves and uses its long arms to catch and eat prey; and the Bosee-Amasee, a half-man, half-fish creature "will see to it that the biggest fish off Andros get on your line if you're nice to him, or not. However, should you displease the Bosee-Amasee it is quite capable of rocking your boat until seasickness forces you to give up, and in extreme cases of displeasure it has been known to capsize large boats."[65] In 1918 Elsie Clews Parsons compiled an extensive work documenting Androsian folktales.[66]

Recreation

Reading as a form of entertainment or recreation is not a part of the culture of Red Bays' children, perhaps due largely to the lack of reading materials. Few homes have books of any kind, except the Bible, and children often asked me for sources to use for book reports due at school. Unfortunately, the "library" that I brought to the field was very limited; books about "research methods" and "fieldwork techniques" were hardly appropriate for their use.

Children in Red Bays entertain themselves with various activities that include games such as ring play, playing church, basketball, volleyball, jack stone or five-rock (a game that uses rocks and a ball or another rock, similar to the American game of jacks), and dominoes. Hand-clapping games, watching television (videos and satellite), and dancing are also favorite pastimes for children and teens.

Some girls learn to make baskets that they can sell to gain some spending money for treats from the shops or for clothing; they wear uniforms to school each day and would like to have nice clothes to show their individual style. The depressed economic conditions in most households make for a limited wardrobe. On several occasions high school children in Red Bays skipped school on "sports day" because they did not have the appropriate "sports outfit" (nice shorts and a top) or the requisite five dollars to donate to the fund-raising effort. This further isolates these children who already suffer from peer harassment about their "backward" community.

Many young people, especially teenagers, complain that there is absolutely nothing to do in Red Bays. When the teens return from high school in Nicholls Town on the school bus, access to many of their friends outside Red Bays is problematic, owing to the lack of transportation. Consequently, there are many times when they stay overnight or longer with a relative or friend's family in another community—Lowe Sound, Fire Road, Mastic Point, or Nicholls Town —and go to school from there. Those who have this alternative consider themselves very fortunate.

Man is an animal suspended in webs
of significance he himself has spun. I
take culture to be those webs, and the
analysis of it to be ... an interpretive
one in search of meaning.

Clifford Geertz

6 ๑๑

Bahamian Black Seminole Identity

The Black Seminoles, now relocated in the Bahamas, confronted new chal-
lenges in a new land. Circumstances once again demanded that they begin the
process of identity renegotiation and cultural adaptation, a process they had
experienced many times since fleeing the plantations of South Carolina and
Georgia. No longer allied with the Seminoles in mutual opposition to Euroamericans, they were instead an isolated group with a common historical
memory, now located on a sparsely populated Out Island of the Bahamas.
Andros afforded unique opportunities to invent new cultural rules, to establish
their own new meaning orders.

Isolated from Bahamian society by their location on the inaccessible northwestern tip of Andros Island, they were primarily concerned with subsistence.
Thanks to the reprieve from British authorities in Nassau, they were free to
draw from the complex of their lived experience and cultural heritage—African, indigenous, Euroamerican—to formulate a new community life in Red
Bays. As the customs officer who "discovered" them in 1828 observed, they were

subsisting on their gardens and the sea; the men farmed the sea, the women and children farmed the land. They remained largely isolated for over one century, but did have some degree of contact with outsiders. Red Bays became a "home base" for spongers who came to harvest the fertile sponge beds on the Mud near Red Bays. With the money they gained from sales to sponge merchants, they purchased flour and other food from Red Bays residents. Exposure to and integration into Bahamian culture gradually increased, especially after the road into the settlement connected it to the outside world in 1968. Despite the increased extralocal influences that the road created for Red Bays, the settlement remains to this day a geographically and culturally isolated, endogamous community. A great deal of change has occurred due to exposure to media, especially U.S. television, which inspires a consumer-oriented lifestyle that culminates in occasional shopping trips to Nassau and Miami. Ironically, Miami is near enough—only a hundred or so miles away—that under certain conditions, the glow of its lights can be seen from the Red Bays dock. But in reality, Miami and Red Bays are worlds apart.

Cultural Identity in the Bahamas

The proclivity to identify with African heritage has undergone a continual evolution in the African diaspora, waxing and waning according to situational—economic, political, and social—forces. Because of the preponderance of erroneous claims about the inferiority of Africans and their culture (much of it gathered without the benefit of any physical presence in Africa or any empirical investigation), many African descended peoples in the Americas were ashamed of Africa—the "Dark Continent"—and wanted to distance themselves from any association with an African heritage. According to Melville J. Herskovits, no group in the United States has "been more completely convinced of the inferior nature of the African background than have the Negroes."[1] This same phenomenon occurred in the Caribbean. Ethnic identity in the Caribbean is heavily shaped by the African experience. Yet Rex Nettleford recognizes that "a major part of the region's cultural difficulties is the persistent denial among many Caribbean people themselves that the African Presence is central to the ethos of the region. Much of what is now 'Caribbean' has indeed been forged in the crucible of the African experience in its myriad encounters with all others for over four centuries."[2]

Creolisation

Nettleford defines creolisation as "the agonising process of renewal and growth that marks the new order of men and women who came originally from different Old World cultures (whether European, African, Levantine, or Oriental) and met in conflict or otherwise on foreign soil."[3] Further, he states that the phenomena of "decolonization (of self and society) and creolization (or indigenization) represent that awesome process actualised in simultaneous acts of negating and affirming, demolishing and constructing, rejecting and reshaping."[4]

The shape of Caribbean identities has been severely modified since the 1960s. The external forces of modernisation, media, and tourism and the internal dynamics created by independence gained in the 1960s and 1970s radically altered societies in the Caribbean. This is the scenario that unfolded in the Bahamas when the black Bahamian majority achieved political gains, riding off the waves of the Civil Rights Movement in the United States.

Historically, Bahamians have not wished to be identified as West Indian, let alone African. Interestingly, the peoples of other Caribbean nations did not consider Bahamians to be West Indians either. The mere fact of Bahamian geographical juxtaposition to Caribbean countries did not make them West Indians, just as their close ties with the United States did not transform Bahamians into North Americans.[5] The lack of identity as West Indians was observed in 1812 by then colonial attorney general William Whylly, who wrote: "I have not been in the West Indies, for the people of this colony do not consider themselves as West Indian."[6] This predilection prevailed even in the twentieth century, and Sir Alan Burns remarked in 1949 that "incidentally, the Bahamians dislike being called West Indians, although no amount of argument can disprove the geographical fact that that the Bahamas are part of the West Indies."[7]

In this sense, the Bahamas is a "world between worlds" because it does not fit neatly into any category. This state of "in-betweenity"[8] causes much consternation among Bahamians, who are sometimes thought of as hybrids, having no particular culture of their own.

Generally, West Indians have been pejoratively characterized by the Bahamian term *grabalicious*.[9] This has led to an association of black assertiveness with the reputedly "primitive" behavior of precolonial Africans, a characterization promoted by white Bahamians. In fact Bahamians "shared to a considerable extent, though for different reasons, the white Bahamians' distrust of West

Indians . . . [who] were generally perceived as snooty like the Barbadians, or quarrelsome like the Jamaicans, and invariably ready to undercut a Bahamian for a job."[10] For this reason, "[i]t has been easier to affirm the Afro-Bahamian identity than to claim to share a common West Indianness."[11]

Despite their dissonance about inclusion in the definition of West Indian, the idea of West Indian identity is beginning to gain acceptance among contemporary Bahamians as a result of the forces of globalization, as well as consciousness-raising about their common legacy of colonization and enslavement. For example, Bahamians have become increasingly involved in Caribbean organizations such as CARICOM (Caribbean Common Market), except in the area of shared currency (the Eastern Caribbean dollar, or EC) because the Bahamian economy is in much better condition than most other CARICOM countries. The Bahamian dollar enjoys parity with that of the United States. Nettleford acknowledges the need for greater cooperation among Caribbean states, suggesting that "[d]espite the diversity of Caribbean life and the surface fragmentation evident in small sovereignties (all with standard bureaucratic rigidities), there are 'submarine' unities manifested in shared cultural identities and sense of community . . . on which functional economic cooperation can be built [for example, CARICOM]."[12]

Generally, the Black Seminole descendants on Andros Island, especially those in Red Bays, are seldom found engaged in discussions of macroeconomics or shared Caribbean identity. Their fundamental concerns have a critical focus on the microeconomic issues of daily survival.

Black Seminole Descendants' Identity

Redemptive ethnography uses the past to redeem the present for the future.[13] The aim of the present work is not redemptive; instead it seeks to interrogate whether these Black Seminole descendants employ this discourse as a tool with which to reinvent their identity and to carve for themselves a place in Bahamian history, thereby creating an oppositional image to the characteristic Bahamian ascription applied to them: backward, uneducated "wild hogs."

This is linked to Foucault's notion of the correlative function of power and knowledge whereby people re-create themselves.[14] In the effort to transform their ascribed identities, they redefine themselves at the micro level by scrutinizing the "politics of everyday life."[15] By means of this process of self-definition—if this is indeed their objective—these Black Seminole descendants can assert a new sense of agency, repositioning themselves in Bahamian society through the construction of a knowledge base, or discourse, about their ancestry. This is a self-actualizing, emergent process.

At a 1988 University of Florida conference, Aimé Césaire spoke about the propensity for self-definition among Afro-Caribbean peoples, stating that "blacks must create a rehabilitation of our values by ourselves, the re-rooting of ourselves within a history, within a geography, within a culture."[16] These sentiments were evident among many residents of Red Bays, predominantly, though, among the community elders.

The intrusion from foreign media—especially television broadcasts from the United States beaming in through the satellite dishes fixed in the yards of many residents—and other effects of modernization and globalization have robbed the younger generations of the opportunities to "talk ol' storee,"[17] the vehicle of cultural transmission that adults in Red Bays had traditionally used to maintain their history and identity. Parables and folklore were passed down through many generations during these sessions.[18] Currently, they self-identify as "Bahamian" but cherish their Black Seminole heritage, indeed employing it as the "cultural capital" they have lacked for such a long time.

The question of identity is centered not only in "roots," but in "routes." As Caribbean scholar Stuart Hall notes:

> Though seeming to originate in an historical past with which they continue to correspond, actually identities are about questions of using the resources of history, language and culture in the process of becoming rather than being: not "who we are" or "where we came from," so much as "what we might become," "how we have been represented" and "how that bears on how we might represent ourselves." . . . Moreover, they emerge within the play of specific modalities of power, and thus are more the product of the marking of difference and exclusion, than they are the sign of an identical, naturally constituted unity.[19]

Overall, the fact of Black Seminole heritage appears essentially a nonissue as far as their status in Bahamian society is concerned. I believe that they may view the publication of their oral history as a means of distinguishing themselves or creating some niche, although they unfailingly consider themselves to be "Bahamian." Almost any Bahamian to whom you mention the name "Black Seminoles" will be able to tell you that "those Indians" live on Andros. However, little more information will be forthcoming because until now that history has been more innuendo than fact. The Black Seminoles of Andros Island were isolated for so long that they were a mystery to most Bahamians; stories about them are mostly the stuff of legend and folklore.

My research indicated that self-defined cultural identity among Black Seminole descendants on Andros Island was invariably "Bahamian."

• Alma Miller: "But when I went over there [Florida] . . . they had told me, say, 'You a Indian.' So I tell them, 'No, I not no Indian, I Bahamian.' He say, 'Yes,' he say, 'look at your bones.' He say, 'Your eye bones is the Indian.' . . . Then, 'Look at your hands,' say, 'they the Indian hands.' So I tell him, I say, 'My foreparents was come from here (Florida), but I a Bahamian.'"[20] Mrs. Miller is one of few Black Seminole descendants on Andros who looks phenotypically Indian; one other is her sister Mary Russell. While Mrs. Miller readily claims her Seminole heritage, and proudly relates the stories told to her by her mother, she emphatically identifies herself as a Bahamian.[21]

• The Reverend Benjamin Lewis: "Like the reaction of the Indian or so, we had no part of that because, my father was just a Bahamian. He just tell us of what he know from his father. And it wasn't no difference from what you see is on today."[22] This account indicates that while the stories were passed down about their history and how they came to be in the Bahamas, they retained no allegiance to their previous lifestyle or identity.

• Charles Bowleg: "We really is Bahamian because any place you were born that's your home, not really Bahamian, Androsian. That's what I call myself because if it's anything, Andros owe me a living, no place else. You can chase me from anyplace else in the world, but when I reach here, I ain't going no further."[23] Here Charles Bowleg makes clear the point that although his ancestors may have come from Florida, his identity and loyalty lie with the only place he has known as home, Andros Island, Bahamas.

When asked whether he considers himself different because of his Seminole ancestry, the Reverend Bertram A. Newton simply replied, "No, we are too much Bahamianize."[24] Black Seminole descendants' sentiments on their personal identity are reflected in the countrywide refrain: "All o' We Is One."

7 ☙

The Meaning of Heritage

Black Seminole heritage is not readily apparent to the casual observer who visits Red Bays. Yet if you ask any resident, she or he will tell you about their Seminole ancestry, or will direct you to one of the community elders, the Reverend Bertram Newton or Mrs. Omelia Marshall, the designated "griots." Thus far there are no overt symbolic references, such as signs or commercial goods and souvenirs; T-shirts, for example, are traditionally a popular way for Bahamians to advertise their political or social proclivities. Gertrude Gibson, the Red Bays entrepreneur who goes out of the community to sell baskets for others, occasionally places inside the baskets a small card that contains some information about the Black Seminole heritage of the people who make them.

Is there some tangible reward for Bahamian Black Seminoles who claim this collective heritage, memory, and identity? Unlike the Black Seminoles or "Freedmen" of Oklahoma, who are currently engaged in a vitriolic dispute with the Seminoles there for inclusion in the reparations package offered to the Seminole Nation of Oklahoma by the United States government, the Black Seminoles of the Bahamas have never expressed any inclination for Seminole tribal

membership. Their inducement is apparently the acquisition of "cultural capital" that may enrich their status among Bahamians, and give them a sense of
empowerment and pride.

The Black Seminole Diaspora

Bahamian Black Seminoles' direct ancestors never joined the westward trek
to Indian Territory, although future research may reveal family ties to some
of the Freedmen. At the time of Removal in 1830, the people through whom
they trace their ancestry had already been resident on Andros Island for nine
years. The Black Seminoles who did accompany their Seminole allies to Indian Territory encountered hostility there from Creek, Cherokee, and other
nations, who viewed them as simply escaped "slaves" and plotted to subject
them once again to chattel slavery—a system which these indigenous nations
had utilized in the Southeast—or sell them to slave-catchers. Intriguing accounts of Black Seminole history after the move westward suggest that the
benign relationship forged in Florida deteriorated significantly as the Seminole–Black Seminole strategic interests ceased to be aligned. Hundreds of
Seminoles and Black Seminoles found these conditions intolerable and subsequently fled Indian Territory, establishing new communities in Texas and
Mexico. Some of their descendants later joined forces with the United States
government and became the Seminole Negro Indian Scouts, ironically, battling
Native Americans in the cause of the United States government. In Brackettville, Texas, descendants of these Seminole Negro Indian Scouts celebrate
their heritage with an annual parade, barbeque, and solemn ceremony at the
cemetery where many of the Scouts are buried. The sponsoring organization
is the Seminole Indian Scouts Cemetery Association (the word "Negro" is no
longer included in the organization's name). The event has speakers from
inside and outside the community: scholars, cowboys, Buffalo soldiers, and
the first African-American Texas Ranger were among the featured guests at
the September 2000 festivities who recounted stories about the courage and
military prowess of the Seminole Indian Scouts.

Cultural Exchange

Recently, I have been involved in plans for a celebration of this unique relationship, a reunion of members of the Seminole Tribe of Florida with members of
the Red Bays community in celebration of their ancestral alliances. In March

2001 two representatives of the Bahamian government and I met with the Seminole Tribe of Florida's international ambassador, Joe Dan Osceola, to plan such a "cultural exchange" event. Plans include cooking and craft demonstrations, music and dancing, all of which may reveal cultural continuities and, if not, will yet be an important acknowledgment of their past. We are excited and optimistic about this historically significant exchange and believe that it will serve as both an acclamation of agency that has been denied both groups for centuries, and a reclamation of shared history that has long suffered from a conspiracy of silence in the historical record. The successful launching of this cultural exchange may herald the invention of a new tradition of friendship and cooperative ventures between the descendants of former allies. Due to fiscal constraints, however, the event, which was originally planned for summer 2001, was postponed.

Our planning activities garnered the curiosity of the Seminole Tribe of Florida's chairman, James Billie, to the extent that he wished to verify the existence of these reputed Seminole "family ties" on Andros Island for himself. A few weeks after my meeting with the Seminole ambassador and Bahamian officials, Chairman Billie flew to Andros unannounced. There he met with several Black Seminole descendants, including the Reverend Bertram A. Newton and Solomon Bowleg (the Bowleg surname is the only remaining one directly linked to the Seminoles).[1] As reported in the *Seminole Tribune,* Chairman Billie's visit was intentionally a surprise because in his words, "You might see me and not know that I am a Seminole, even though I speak my language fluently. But I did not want to come over like that so that you might, for the lack of a better word, 'bullshit' me. We needed to make sure this was all true." Chairman Billie was concerned about whether the Bahamian Black Seminoles are seeking inclusion into the Seminole Tribe, and all the benefits that membership would accrue. The *Tribune* article notes that "[g]enerations of intermarriage have thinned the Andros Island Seminoles' bloodline far beyond the quantum necessary for membership in the Seminole Tribe of Florida." The planned cultural exchange and reunion was never intended as a conduit for tribal membership. As the Reverend Mr. Newton confirmed to Chairman Billie during his impromptu visit, "No such agenda exists."

Vital Oral Tradition

The oral tradition of the Black Seminoles of the Bahamas exists not only among the people of Red Bays but among descendants in other Andros Island communities as well. In 1972, scholar and self-described "inveterate wanderer" Jan Carew encountered an elderly woman in an unidentified Andros Island community, a Black Seminole descendant who recalled to him that

> I heard 'bout the battle of Swannee against Stonewall Jackson, my grandmother tell me 'bout it and her grandmother tell her 'bout it long before. Stories like that does come down to us with voices in the wind.... She tell me how the Old Ones used to talk 'bout the look on them white soldiers faces when they see Black fighters looking like they grow outta the swamp grass and the hammocks, coming at them with gun and cutlass. Jackson get hurt at Swannee, man. The ancestors brutalize him there. . . . Oh God! That man Jackson was cruel, eh? He make slaves of them who was free already for two and three generation. He sell the grandchildren of former slaves to the grandchildren of former slave owners! My old face beat against eighty-odd years. . . . But when Jesus of Nazareth decide to send Mantop to carry me to the Great Beyond, wherever my blood-seed scatter, they will spread the word 'bout how Black and Seminole ancestors fight side by side at Swannee."[2]

The fact that this history has survived numerous generations demonstrates that the historical relationship with the Seminole Indians of Florida is a critical element in the crucible of Bahamian Black Seminole identity construction and is cogent testimony to the meaning of heritage.

Distorting racial history . . . injures
dark children. They live with a
muted heritage. Despite Black Indian
contributions to this land, neither
Black nor Indian children nor their
parents have an awareness of this
legacy. . . . Further, they divide people
today who could benefit from unity.

William L. Katz

8 ☙

Conclusion

The present ethnohistorical account explores the intricate and intimate in-
terrelationship of an indigenous people—the Seminoles—and Africans, two
peoples whose histories are intimately intertwined yet have been obscured in
the conventional historical record. Both were systematically subjected to physical and psychological subjugation and genocide by various factions of Europeans during their conquest of the New World. Seminoles and Black Seminoles
manipulated and negotiated the means to survive and transcend the devastating impact of European hegemony.

Their journey from the plantations in North America ultimately led a few of
the Black Seminoles to the Bahamas, where they finally secured the freedom for
which they and their ancestors had fought and died for over a hundred years.
It is my hope that this research will make an important addition to New World
history and will stimulate interest in further research that will help to heal the
traditional historical record's chronic condition of structural amnesia.

Black Seminole descendants on Andros Island, and those who migrated elsewhere in the Bahamas, enjoy an extraordinary and unique legacy, one that distinguishes them from other Bahamians. Their ancestors bequeathed a tradition of resistance and survival against the odds that in many ways remains evident in the contemporary community of Red Bays. Their path diverged from that of the majority of Black Seminoles in Florida, who were either forced on the Trail of Tears to Indian Territory with their Seminole allies, or were reclaimed by their former "masters." Black Seminoles in Florida were in imminent danger of reenslavement as Euroamericans persistently encroached southward in Florida, seizing and settling the land occupied by Seminoles and their Black Seminole allies. Confronted with the constant danger of recapture, and denied the earlier-pledged assistance from their British "allies" in the Bahamas who had promised to defend their interests against Euroamerican aggressors, they sailed across the Gulf Stream waters in dugout canoes and wreckers, an undeniably formidable endeavor.

The forces of globalization and modernization are increasingly evident and have been the catalysts for tremendous sociocultural change in Red Bays. The most significant of these changes was perhaps the construction of a road in 1968 that literally and figuratively served as a "bridge" to the outside world. For the first time in the residents' 150-year presence, Red Bays became accessible by vehicle, rather than solely by boat or footpaths through the pineyard. The unpaved road, a factor that still presented an obstacle to easy accessibility, was finally paved in the late 1980s. For the first time, Red Bays children had the opportunity to go beyond grade six, the limit at their own primary school; they now attend North Andros High School in Nicholls Town, where, ironically, the school's mascot name is the Seminoles.

Additional significant changes were made to the infrastructure of Red Bays—most of these implemented within the past ten years: electricity, a dedicated water pump and, most recently, telephone service in individual homes. Prior to December 1998 residents had access to telephone service only at a central BATELCO (Bahamas Telephone Corporation) location. The latter "improvement" has had a perhaps unanticipated impact on the cultural ecology of Red Bays; the primary incomes of two Red Bays families as well as the central meeting place have been eliminated.

Conversion to a primarily cash economy—and perhaps the wider exposure provided by high school and media—compels young men and women in far greater numbers than their predecessors to seek employment opportunities available almost exclusively in the capital city, Nassau. The lack of opportunities "down home" is a predicament they share with many other Family Island Bahamians.

Although physically located a mere twenty-five miles across the sea from Andros Island, Nassau is a vastly different place. For the people of Red Bays, a community that affords a relaxed, though economically impoverished, existence, where few people lock their doors, where conflicts are settled by fists and harsh words rather than guns, and where residents have to travel twenty miles to the nearest settlement, the adaptation to a fast-paced and crowded Nassau lifestyle is daunting.

Contemporary life in Nassau is likened in a popular Bahamian song to living in "sardine cans," where all food and water are imported, and where people can no longer sleep soundly without bars on their windows. This depiction may seem extreme, but, unfortunately, it does accurately portray life for many people in this city that suffers from overpopulation. Most tourists never notice the serious problems in this city because their visits are most often restricted to the traditional tourist areas: Bay Street and Paradise Island. Over 65 percent of the total Bahamian population of 304,000 currently resides on New Providence Island, most of them in Nassau. Another 15 percent of the population lives on Grand Bahama Island, site of the Bahamas' second-largest tourist destination, Freeport. The remainder of the population is spread throughout thirty Family Islands, many of which are sparsely populated.

New Providence Island covers approximately eighty square miles (versus the nearly 2,300 square miles of Andros) and is one of the smallest of the occupied islands in the Bahamian archipelago. For black Bahamians in particular, the influences of modern society, media exploitation, and subjection to subordinate status in their own country (due in part to the exigencies of a tourist-driven economy) have all served to create a national atmosphere that is increasingly volatile. Economic diversification and redistribution of development projects to benefit the Family Islands would be a blessing for the people there, and may also be the salvation of the tourism business in Nassau, where conditions—for both Bahamians and tourists—have deteriorated.

Traditions in Red Bays have changed significantly. Red Bays residents' ancestors had a more intimate relationship with both the land and the sea. While current residents continue to use the sea as a subsistence strategy, their relationship to the land has changed dramatically. Despite the fact that Andros Island possesses the largest tract of arable land in the country, the farming tradition has ended, a factor that has significantly altered the communal dynamic of the settlement where the majority of residents traditionally traveled by boat once every year to spend six months farming a large tract of land in Billy Coppitt.

Men and, infrequently, women may go out to sea to catch dinner, or the men harvest sponges to sell to the local sponge merchant for cash. Often the money obtained from sponging or the infrequent "big catch" is spent on consecutive nights of drinking until the money has been completely exhausted. They own only small fishing boats, which are not seaworthy enough to withstand even modest winds on the high seas; this creates a precarious scenario for daily subsistence. Opportunities presented by other lucrative "informal" economic strategies, especially in the 1980s, significantly influenced the shift of emphasis from farming and fishing.

The long-standing tradition of "sewing baskets" has not lost its emphasis in Red Bays. The sale of baskets remains a vital subsistence strategy, engaged in by most women in the settlement as well as by a few men. Red Bayans' unique style of basketry, a style that bears an unmistakable resemblance to the traditional styles of both the Sea Islands of South Carolina and the West Coast of Africa, is instantly recognizable to other Bahamians as "Red Bays' baskets." These baskets command a premium price in marketplaces across the Bahamas.

Research Questions and Answers

The primary objectives of my research in Red Bays were to record the oral history about the community's connections to the Florida Seminoles and to obtain answers to questions of cultural identity, both how these Black Seminole descendants have formulated their own identities and how other Bahamians define them.

Is there still a strong identification with either Indian or African ancestry among Black Seminole descendants in the Andros community? No longer influenced by adjacent communities of Seminole Indians, Black Seminoles who escaped to the Bahamas settled into a new identity as Bahamians. They cling to the proud legacy of their ancestors who resisted enslavement and braved the Gulf Stream waters in canoes to find freedom in Red Bays on "The Promised (Is)Land" of Andros. Yet they unequivocally identify with the only home they have known, the Bahamas.

If the population does not identify with either heritage—Seminole or African—why not, and with what have they replaced such an identification? Their daily existence and surface consciousness does not contemplate complex associations with African or Seminole heritage. They identify simply as Bahamians who happen to have a unique ancestry that they enjoy talking about to visitors, but that plays little or no active role in their daily lives.

Is there evidence of cultural traits identifiable from either Indian or African ancestry, or a fusion of both, in the language, religious customs, crafts, livelihood strategies, and social structure in these settlements today? Although there are remnants of Seminole cultural traditions and significant instances of African cultural traditions, the Black Seminole descendants in Red Bays and in other settlements of Andros Island do not consciously identify their culture as such. The livelihood and subsistence strategies they employ are simply viewed as their "Bahamian" way of life.

I concede that some of the above questions come precariously close to a cultural essentialist argument. It is clear that merely searching for static cultural "traits" or material culture does not provide insight into the deeper underlying issues of cultural identity and cultural retentions. The experience of living on Andros Island for one year, spending the majority of that time in the settlement of Red Bays, helped me to discover that what has been preserved is not necessarily tangibly evident, but is, rather, epistemological—a complex of knowledge, beliefs, and ways of knowing that derive from the synthesis of heritage and adaptation.

So what, in the final analysis, is the significance of their history to their contemporary conceptualization of identity and their everyday lives? Well, a review of their history is testimony to a nonessentialist view of identity as "an ever-changing process which always leaves something 'outside' because of its very nature of being in a state of constant change and flux based upon opposition to some 'other.' It is an act of power."[1] Their contemporary conceptualization of identity is premised upon the necessity of adaptation to a Bahamian culture that is in the throes of adjustment to the forces of globalization. Identity construction is contextual; Africans in the New World diaspora have repeatedly had to renegotiate their identities in the diverse contexts into which they have been thrust. The Black Seminoles and their descendants are no exception.

Notes

Introduction

1. See Mulroy 1993: 26; Porter 1996: 26.

2. See Harrison and Harrison 1999.

3. Only recently has the American Anthropological Association of issued a "Statement on Race" that repudiates the biological basis of "race."

4. *Womanist* is the term I prefer to use rather than *feminist*, to avoid the negative connotations associated with the latter term.

5. LaFlamme 1985. LaFlamme's research site was on an island that had a mixed population of white and black Bahamians with a reputed "Yankee culture."

6. Hughes 1981: 72.

7. Cox 1971: 361.

8. McClaurin 1996; Harrison 1991; Whitehead 1980.

9. Hurston 1942: 263.

10. Mead and Métraux 1953.

11. Hurston 1942: 45.

Chapter 1. The Significance of African and Indigenous Peoples' Contacts in the Americas

1. Hudson 1971: 1.

2. Forbes 1993; Woodson 1920.

3. Here the term *consent* means that people are educated to the point to which they

---

believe or internalize erroneous definitions of themselves, concepts of proper behavior, and "common sense," which are dictated by the dominant group.

4. Clarke 1957: 75.

5. Katz 1986: 10.

6. Zinn 1980: 16.

7. Simmons offers a romanticized explanation for the demise of Native American peoples, stating that "[t]he awful and swift destruction which took place among them after the Spanish conquest, was not the result of the labors imposed on them . . . but it was solely the subjection of their spirit, the bitter cup of humiliation, drugged by servitude, that produced their speedy depopulation." Simmons 1973: 58.

8. Higginbotham 1978: 116.

9. Curtin 1994.

10. Robinson 1971.

11. Ibid.

12. Higginbotham 1978: 394–95.

13. Ibid.

14. Williams 1944: 14.

15. Conniff and Davis 1994: 127.

16. Ibid.

17. Littlefield 1981.

18. Ibid.

19. The regional origin of enslaved Africans, as indicated on traders' records, was not entirely reliable. Although the captive African may have embarked from a specific port, she or he may actually have originated from the interior.

20. These valuations were also used to calculate policy premiums for insurance against mortality on the slave ships during the Middle Passage (Littlefield 1981).

21. They left with the British for the British Caribbean Islands as well as Nova Scotia.

22. Joyner 1984.

23. Aptheker 1979 [1939]: 2.

24. Ibid.: 151, 165.

25. Craton 1982. The latter scenario describes what transpired in Florida between the Seminole Indians and the Africans who were fleeing enslavement on the plantations of Georgia and the Carolinas.

26. Price 1979: 3.

27. Katz 1986: 40; also see Price 1979.

28. Katz 1986: 46. According to Katz, the name Ganga-Zumba means "Great Ruler."

29. Aptheker 1979 [1939].

30. Ibid.

31. Katz 1986. Some maroons also struck agreements to return runaways as a means to ensure their own safety.

Chapter 2. New Identities, New Alliances

1. Ramos 1957: 175.

2. Baker 1998: 30–31.

3. Feagin and Feagin 1999: 83.

4. Du Bois 1962 [1935]: 19.

5. Cf. Geertz 1973.

6. Sithole 1986; Paranjpe 1986.

7. William Sturtevant introduced this term in his 1971 seminal essay "Creek into Seminole."

8. Although the term *tribe* is held by many scholars and others to be pejorative, especially when referring to Africans, it is freely employed by some ethnic groups. One such group is the Seminole Tribe of Florida, Inc.

9. Hill 1996: 1.

10. English traders coined the term *Creek*. Its origin has been variously attributed to the proximity of these Native Americans to numerous rivers and streams and to the Muskogees' having lived along the Ochesee Creek. The Muskogees were called Ochesees by the Hitchitis after they invaded and settled on Hitchiti land.

11. Littlefield 1977.

12. Swanton 1998 [1922]: 216.

13. Moore 1996.

14. Swanton 1998 [1922]: 225.

15. Miller 1997: 15.

16. Carew 1992.

17. Miller 1997: 15.

18. The Yamassee War, instigated by Lower Creeks against the Carolina traders, was fought from 1715 to 1716. The Yamassees were virtually destroyed; many were sold into slavery in Jamaica and New England, their towns removed to Guale (an area along the Georgia coast from the Savannah River to St. Andrews Sound) and Florida.

19. Miller 1997: 16.

20. Ibid.

21. Giddings 1858: 3.

22. Franco 1968: 93; see also Guillot 1961: 38.

23. Giddings 1858.

24. Katz 1986; Littlefield 1977.

25. Sturtevant 1971: 110.

26. Littlefield 1977.

27. Hudson 1971: 121.

28. Landers 1996.

29. Landers has conducted extensive research in this area. She mentions (1996: 94) the names of two free blacks, Abraham McQueen and Sequi, who filed claims against the U.S. government for damages incurred as a result of the Patriot War of 1812. These names can be found among the roster listing ninety-seven "foreign Negro slaves" who were discovered to be living in Red Bays, Andros Island, Bahamas, in 1828. See Wood 1980: 9.

30. The enslaved had legal remedies to escape cruel masters and ensure their personal security, as well as own and transfer property. Landers 1996: 18.

31. They were paid very well for this: one musket and three blankets for the return of one fugitive slave (one musket alone would normally cost thirty-five deerskins, which would usually take several months of hunting to acquire). Hudson 1971: 36.

32. Hill 1996: 4–5.

33. Porter 1996: 9.

34. However, not all Seminoles were friendly toward the runaway Africans.

35. Porter 1996: 6.

36. Joyner 1984.

37. Windley 1983: 109.

38. Ibid.

39. See Swanton 1946.

40. Porter 1971: 44.

41. Ibid.

42. Gad Humphreys, quoted in Klos 1989: 66.

43. Klos 1989: 60.

44. Ibid.: 55.

45. Ranger 1988: 248.

46. Shaw 1995: 6.

47. Hall 1996.

48. The integrity of the family was often sustained by slaveholders in the Caribbean. Slaveholder Thomas Spalding also found this an advantageous strategy on his Georgia Sea Island plantation, Sapelo.

49. Wright 1986: 277.

50. Herron 1994; Weisman 2000.

51. Simmons 1973 [1822]: 76. My emphases.

52. Miller 1997: 65.

53. Mulroy 1993.

54. Herron 1994: 38.

55. Bartram 1996 [1791]: 37–39.

56. "July" is a common surname among descendants of the Seminole Negro Indian

Scouts who currently reside in Brackettville, Texas. The Seminole Negro Indian Scouts were formerly Black Seminoles who moved westward with the Seminoles at the time of Removal. They escaped from Indian Territory, settled in Mexico, and later agreed to fight for the U.S. government against Indians in the Southwest.

57. Littlefield 1977; Weisman 2000.

58. Mulroy 1993; Price 1979.

59. Quoted in Herron 1994: 40–41.

60. Herron 1994: 70.

61. Weik (in press).

62. McCall 1974 [1868].

63. Mykel 1962; Herron 1994.

64. I have been told by some Seminoles that occasionally, outsiders have been invited to the Green Corn Dance ceremony. These have traditionally been limited to non-Indian spouses of tribal members and the occasional anthropologist, to whom they sometimes gave incorrect information to "throw [him/her] off."

65. Windley 1983.

66. Klos 1989: 69.

67. Ibid.: 69–70.

68. Miller 1997: 65–66.

69. R. Bateman, quoted in Miller 1997: 208.

70. Katz 1986.

71. King Payne was the nephew of Cowkeeper, leader of the Alachua band of Seminoles. He took over leadership after Cowkeeper's death in the 1790s (Herron 1994: 36). King Payne died in 1813 after suffering injuries in a battle with the Georgia militia.

72. Spain then retained control until 1819.

73. Katz 1986: 54.

74. Porter 1996: 16.

75. Carew 1988: 5.

76. The annexation was officially ratified in 1821.

77. Landers 1996.

78. Ibid.: 96–97.

79. Porter 1996: 27.

80. Potter 1836: 14.

81. Klos 1989: 57.

82. Littlefield 1977: 12; see also Porter 1996.

83. Porter 1996: 33. Porter notes that John Caesar recruited runaways and freed blacks from the St. Augustine area to their cause of resisting removal.

84. Carew 1988: 11.

85. Osceola died in captivity.

86. Potter 1836: 14, 16–17.

87. Ibid.: 17.

88. Littlefield 1977: 11.

89. Richardson n.d.

90. Littlefield 1977: 15.

91. Ibid.: 15–16. According to Littlefield, this last category was highly disputed.

92. Ibid.

Chapter 3. The Promised Island: Andros, Bahamas

1. *Bahamas Royal Gazette* 1819b.

2. Porter 1945.

3. Ibid.: 58.

4. Munnings 1819. This may have been an alternative spelling for Chief King Heijah (also known as Koe Hadjo or Kenhadjo, also known as Coa Hadjo, and also known as Alligator), who was listed as a resident of Negro Town in Florida, occupied primarily by runaway Africans (Swanton 1953; Mykel 1962).

5. *Bahamas Royal Gazette* 1819b.

6. Munnings 1819.

7. Neill 1952: 65–66. The Seminoles were skilled at building large dugout canoes that could carry twenty to thirty people and were suitable for crossing wide expanses of sea.

8. Grant 1821.

9. Ibid.

10. Goggin 1946.

11. Bethell 1828.

12. Quoted in Flagg 2000.

13. Hursh n.d.

14. Shortly before the March 1997 Bahamian General Elections, the island's political divisions were reduced to two—North Andros and South Andros—but Androsians still maintain the three distinctions.

15. Randolph 1994: 243; Saunders 1994 [1990]; Cash, Gordon, and Saunders 1991.

16. Vansina 1985: 13.

17. Finnegan 1992: 48.

18. Abercrombie 1998.

19. Vansina 1985: 17.

20. Joseph Lewis's grandfather's name was listed on the 1828 customs roster as "Sam Louis."

21. Bertram A. Newton, interview by author, tape recording, Red Bays, November

12, 1996. Subsequent quotations of Bertram Newton in this chapter are from this interview.

22. Benjamin Lewis, interview by author, tape recording, Red Bays, November 12, 1996.

23. *Sewing* is the term Red Bayans use when describing how they weave baskets.

24. William Colebrooke, interview by author, tape recording, Red Bays, November 12, 1996.

25. Frederick Russell, interview by author, tape recording, Red Bays, February 4, 1997.

26. *Cutlass* is the term Bahamians use for a machete.

27. Alma (Prudence) Miller, interview by author, tape recording, Lowe Sound, March 7, 1997.

28. Charles Bowleg, interview by author, tape recording, Nicholls Town, February 24, 1997. Subsequent quotations of Bowleg in this chapter are from this interview.

29. Omelia Marshall, interview by author, tape recording, Red Bays, November 21, 1996.

30. Forfar Field Station is a marine biology field school for U.S. high school students and teachers, located in Blanket Sound, Central Andros.

31. Omelia Marshall interview.

32. Saunders 1985: 17.

33. Commonwealth 1984: 11–12.

34. Northrop 1910: 14.

35. The 2nd West India Regiment in the Bahamas consisted of Africans recruited from British territories and liberated Africans. "The Bahamian white inhabitants were not happy with the fact that hundreds of blacks were being used to garrison these islands and as far back as 1801, showed their resentment and distaste by illtreating the soldiers, and demanding that the Home Government remove them from New Providence. They were severely afraid that if the freed Negroes, slaves, and troops banded together, the type of Negro slave revolution which occurred in Haiti in the 1790s could happen in the Bahamas." Commonwealth 1984: 22.

36. Bahamas Department of Archives 1989: 21. The report of the planned revolt is contained in a letter, Dunmore to Portland, May 10, 1795. CO23/34/45.

37. Williams 1979.

38. Collinwood 1989a: 11.

39. Manwaring 1928; Commonwealth 1984.

40. Commonwealth 1984: 8.

41. This settlement was most probably named in honor of a Colonel Nichols, a British officer with whom some of the refugees had served in the War of 1812, and who established Negro Fort.

42. Marion Pickstock, interview by Dr. Gail Saunders, tape recording, March 4, 1980. Bahamas Department of Archives, Nassau.

43. Grant to Barthurst. June 30, 1828. Document. Governor's Despatches. Bahamas Department of Archives, Nassau. CO23/78/58.

44. Bethell to Controller of Customs, London. October 30, 1828. Governor's Office, Secretary of State Papers. Bahamas Department of Archives, Nassau.

45. "Slave Registers, 1821–1834," microfilm, Bahamas Department of Archives, Nassau.

46. Commonwealth 1974: 20.

47. Bethell to Controller of Customs, London. October 30, 1828. Document. Governor's Office, Secretary of State Papers. Bahamas Department of Archives, Nassau.

48. Twiss to Downing Street, London. February 21, 1829. Document. Governor's Despatches. Bahamas National Archives, Nassau.

49. Grant 1828.

50. Smyth 1831.

51. Bethell 1831.

52. Williams 1979.

53. Barthurst 1828.

54. Smyth 1831.

55. B. B. Dean and W. L. Roe, to Treasury Chambers. February 11, 1829. Letter. Bahamas Department of Archives, Nassau.

56. Smyth 1831.

Chapter 4. "We Reach": Bahamaland

1. This refers to the Bahamas National Anthem: "Lift up your head, to the rising sun, Bahamaland. / March on to glory, your bright banners waving high. / See how the world marks the manner of your bearing. / Pledge to excel through love and unity. / Pressing onward, march together, to a common loftier goal; / Steady sunward, tho' the weather hide the wide and treacherous shoal. / Lift up your head to the rising sun Bahamaland. / 'Til the road you've trod, lead unto your God. / March on, Bahamaland."

2. Aarons 1990.

3. Peggs 1957 [1928].

4. Aarons 1990.

5. Commonwealth 1984: 9.

6. Saunders 1983.

7. Abaco was the Bahamian island advertised most widely as suitable for British Loyalists' resettlement after the 1783 Treaty of Paris between Spain and Britain ceded Florida to the Spaniards. On Abaco the Loyalists formed the settlement of Carleton, named after Sir Guy Carleton, who had been the commander-in-chief of British

forces in America. Bahamas Department of Archives. "The Bahamas in the Age of Revolution 1775–1848." 1989: 8.

8. LaFlamme 1985: 9

9. Cash, Gordon, and Saunders 1991: 49–50.

10. *An Account of All Cotton Plantations in the Bahamas,* November 1, 1785. CO23/30/335, Bahamas Department of Archives. "The coming of the American Refugees boosted the economic situation in the colony as they introduced cotton cultivation previously grown in Georgia. Later Anguilla cotton, a long staple cotton which grew all year round was cultivated. By 1778 cotton production had become a successful operation with over 8,000 acres of land under cultivation. Between 1784–1790 the cotton yield equaled £27,393.1s.3d in value. The best cotton islands proved to be the Turks and Caicos Islands, Long Island, Watlings Island, Cat Island and Exuma." Commonwealth 1989: 9.

11. Before the passage of Loyalist vagrancy and racial separation laws, housing for white and black Bahamians was intermingled throughout Nassau. Saunders 1983: 45.

12. Robert Curry, quoted in Wood 1980: 18, appendix 24.

13. Governor's Despatches, 1827–31, Bahamas Department of Archives.

14. Interestingly, the first "coloured man" was elected to the House of Assembly on the very same date.

15. *Royal Gazette,* July 16, 1834, p. 3, quoted in Commonwealth 1984: 43.

16. Smyth was dismissed as governor of the Bahamas in 1833 and took up the same position in British Guiana. He died there in 1834. Wood 1990: 22.

17. Hughes 1981: 6–7.

18. Mintz 1985.

19. Johnson 1991; Saunders 1985; Knight 1997.

20. Harrison 1995: 47.

21. Collinwood 1989b: 10.

22. A "lick-o'-de-brush" refers to having some African ancestry.

23. Hypodescent is otherwise referred to as the "one drop rule": if a person has one drop of African blood, they are considered "black" (Harris 1964). According to Harris, "[t]his rule of hypodescent is ... an invention which we in the United States have made in order to keep biological facts from intruding into our collective racist fantasies." Harris 1964: 56

24. Wood 1990: 22.

25. Quoted in Dodge 1989: 53.

26. Defries 1929: 18–19.

27. Saunders 1983.

28. Bacot 1869, quoted in Hughes 1981.

29. Wood 1990: 22.

30. Hughes 1989, 1981. See also Saunders 1994 [1990] and 1993.

31. Dodge 1989; Hughes 1989.

32. Collinwood 1989b.

33. Wilson 1989: 81.

34. Smith 1988: 147.

35. Collinwood and Dodge 1989b; LaFlamme 1985.

36. Payne 1993: 68.

37. Collinwood 1989b: 18–19.

38. Hughes 1989; see also Edelman 1972.

39. Free National Movement 1997: 4.

40. Maingot 1994: 229.

41. Hubert Ingraham, election campaign speech at North Andros High School, Nicholls Town, Andros, Bahamas, February 20, 1997.

42. This strategy has been implemented in other Caribbean countries with varying degrees of success. If there is no "value added," the benefits reaped by the host country are few, and wages are very low.

43. Collinwood 1989a: 7.

44. Collinwood and Dodge 1989: 103.

45. Edie 1991.

46. Deveaux 1997.

47. See Edie 1991.

48. Maingot 1994: 231.

49. Free National Movement 1997.

Chapter 5. De People Dem: Black Seminoles in the "Land behind God's Back"

1. Burnside 1867.

2. Ibid.: 17.

3. Wood 1980: 18.

4. Newton 1968: 1.

5. Goggin 1946: 201.

6. Tellis Smith, interview by author, tape recording, Mastic Point, April 3, 1997.

7. Marion Pickstock, interview by Dr. Gail Saunders, March 4, 1980.

8. Between the mid nineteenth century and the early twentieth century, many Bahamians migrated to Florida to work, primarily as domestics, in the growing tourist industry there.

9. Cash, Gordon, and Saunders 1991: 49–50.

10. Moseley 1926: 66.

11. *Nassau Magazine* 1938.

12. Robert Curry, quoted in Wood 1980: 18, appendix 24.

13. Andros has often been referred to as the "Big Yard" because the island represents 43 percent of the total acreage of the Bahamas and its largest tract of arable land. It is also referred to as the "Sleeping Giant" because the island's substantial natural and human resources have long remained latent. Deveaux 1997; Albury 1975.

14. Commonwealth 1984: 21.

15. Pickstock, interview.

16. Curry, quoted in Wood 1980: 18, appendix 24.

17. Marshall, interview, 1996.

18. Newton 1968: 3.

19. Ibid.

20. Logan 1969.

21. The first road was the catalyst for Bertram Newton's publication of the pamphlet *A History of Red Bays, Andros, Bahamas* in 1968. As he states, "The road was officially declared open by the Company [Owens Illinois Company, also known as Bahamas Agricultural Industries, Ltd.] at ceremonies held at Red Bays on August 3rd, 1968, when two hundred visitors came." Newton 1968: 4.

22. Several older residents expressed that the thatch camps (or thatch huts) were warmer and safer in storms than "flat board" houses.

23. See Frazier 1966 [1939]; Smith 1988; Safa 1995; Herskovits 1958 [1941]; Gonzalez 1984; Clarke 1957; Simey 1946; McKenzie 1993; Braithwaite 1973; etc.

24. Smith 1988; see also Leach 1961; Schneider 1984.

25. Schusky 1983: 15.

26. Berlin and Rowland 1997: 3.

27. Smith 1988: 121.

28. Gonzalez 1984: 7. The Garifuna, descendants of Carib Indians and Africans, live in Belize, Panama, and other areas of Central America.

29. Smith 1988: 56.

30. The following quotation from Bascom illuminates a similarly tight mother-child bond among Gullah families in the Sea Islands of South Carolina and Georgia: "In the structure of the Gullah family there seems to be a certain matrilineal emphasis for which there are counterparts in Africa. For example, there is the feeling that an individual is somehow more closely related to his mother than to his father. There are several rationalizations for this, but one is the same as that offered in Africa, namely that a person is fed on his mother's milk." Bascom 1941: 48.

31. Smith 1988: 345; see also Safa 1986: 5.

32. McKenzie 1993: 76.

33. *Sweetheart* is the term used for an extramarital partner.

34. Smith 1988: 147.

35. Twining and Baird 1991: 5.

36. Otterbein 1963: 176.

37. Safa 1986: 10.

38. Massiah 1986: 103.

39. Otterbein 1963: 131.

40. Pocock 1971.

41. Page 1993: 80.

42. McClaurin 1996: 21.

43. Ingraham, election campaign speech, February 20, 1997.

44. Safa 1986: 12.

45. Newton, interview, 1996.

46. MacCormack and Draper 1987: 143.

47. Richardson n.d.: 1–28. Richardson goes on to state: "Some of the better-looking women were sometimes mated with master or overseers; this resulted in the much-sought mulatto Negroes who were used as house slaves. In many cases the mulattoes were thought to be good for little else besides work around the houses; in others they were taught to keep records and supervise the work of other slaves."

48. MacCormack and Draper 1987: 146–47.

49. Otterbein 1963: 104.

50. *Report on Visit to Andros Fibre Plantation of Mr. Chamberlain,* 1894, Series V15 N1, pp. 1–7, Bahamas Department of Archives.

51. Goggin 1937.

52. The "false economy" created by extensive drug trafficking led to an inverse ratio of work to profit that now discourages harder work for smaller returns, such as those gained from farming.

53. Collinwood 1989b: 12.

54. Otterbein 1963: 182.

55. See Brodber 1975.

56. Twining and Baird 1991: 4–5.

57. Marshall, interview, 1996.

58. See Safa 1995: 39.

59. Other residents complain that while they were off island building materials were "tiefed" by neighbors and were never replaced.

60. Omelia Marshall, interview by author, Red Bays, May 1, 1997.

61. William Colebrooke, interview by author, tape recording, Red Bays, April 25, 1997.

62. Moseley 1926: 66.

63. Rawnsley 1961.

64. Daisy gives lectures on Seminole culture and history at universities and at the

Ah-Tah-Thi-Ki Museum on the Big Cypress Reservation, where she resides. She is the great-granddaughter of Chief Jumper, a Seminole who refused to leave Florida for Indian Territory. Chief Jumper is reputed to have killed Major Dade in the Seminole Wars.

65. *Nassau Magazine* 1958.

66. Parsons 1918.

Chapter 6. Bahamian Black Seminole Identity

1. Herskovits 1941: 31.

2. Nettleford 1970.

3. Ibid.: 2.

4. Ibid.: 181.

5. Collinwood 1989b.

6. Whylly, quoted in Johnson 1991: vi.

7. Burns, quoted in Johnson 1991: vi.

8. Best 1996.

9. Wilson 1989: 87. The term *grabalicious* connotes greedy and/or arrogant behavior.

10. Ibid.: 87.

11. Hughes 1989: 88.

12. Nettleford 1970: x.

13. Shaw 1995: 13.

14. Layder 1994.

15. Ibid.

16. Young 1993: 14.

17. Parsons described the practice of "ol' storee" as follows: "You *talk* ol' storee ... almost anywhere I could get a group of women and children around me eager to talk 'ol' storee' for a penny or two. ... But the best way to hear the stories is in the evening, the time when they are wont to be told." Parsons 1918: x.

18. Ibid.

19. Hall 1996: 4.

20. Miller, interview.

21. Porter encountered a similar propensity from a Black Seminole descendant in Brackettville, Texas, who said, "We's cullud people. I don't say we don't has no Injun blood, 'cause we has. But we ain't no Injuns. We's cullud people." *The Negro on the American Frontier* 1971: 3.

22. Lewis, interview.

23. Bowleg, interview.

24. Newton, interview.

Chapter 7. The Meaning of Heritage

1. The story of this historically noteworthy encounter is reported in the *Seminole Tribune,* vol. 22, no. 5, April 13, 2001.

2. Carew 1988: 5.

Chapter 8. Conclusion

1. Hall 1996: 5.

Bibliography

Aarons, G. A. 1990. The Prehistory and Early History of Andros: A Summary Report as Consultant Archaeologist/Anthropologist. Bahamas Department of Archives.

Abercrombie, Thomas A. 1998. *Pathways of Memory and Power: Ethnography and History Among an Andean People*. Madison: University of Wisconsin Press.

Albury, Paul. 1975. *The Story of the Bahamas*. London: Macmillan.

Aptheker, Herbert. 1979 [1939]. Maroons within the Present Limits of the United States. In *Maroon Societies: Rebel Slave Communities in the Americas*, by Richard Price, 151–67. Baltimore: Johns Hopkins University Press.

Bahamas Department of Archives. 1989. "The Bahamas in the Age of Revolution, 1775–1848." Nassau, Bahamas.

Bahamas Royal Gazette. October 2, 1819. In *A Guide to Selected Sources for the History of the Seminole Settlements at Red Bays, Andros 1917–1980*, by David E. Wood, appendix 3. Nassau, Bahamas: Department of Archives.

Baker, Lee D. 1998. *From Savage to Negro: Anthropology and the Construction of Race, 1896–1954*. Berkeley: University of California Press.

Barthurst, Earl. 1828. Document. Governor's Despatches. CO23 1700s–1900s. Barthurst to Governor Cameron. July 31, 1828.

Bartram, William. 1996 [1791]. *Travels through North and South Carolina*. Philadelphia: James and Johnson.

Bascom, William R. 1941. Acculturation among the Gullah Negroes. *American Anthropologist* 43.

Bateman, Rebecca. 1990. Africans and Indians: A Comparative Study of the Black Carib and Black Seminole. *Ethnohistory* 37:1 (winter).

Berlin, Ira, and Leslie S. Rowland, eds. 1997. *Families and Freedom: A Documentary History of African-American Kinship in the Civil War Era.* New York: New Press.

Best, Lloyd. 1996. In-Betweenity. Paper presented at Conference on Caribbean Culture, University of the West Indies, Mona, Jamaica.

Bethell, Winer. 1828. London Duplicate Despatches. In *A Guide to Selected Sources for the History of the Seminole Settlements at Red Bays, Andros 1917–1980,* by David E. Wood, appendix 10. Nassau, Bahamas: Department of Archives.

———. 1831. London Duplicate Despatches. In *A Guide to Selected Sources for the History of the Seminole Settlements at Red Bays, Andros 1917–1980,* by David E. Wood, appendix 12. Nassau, Bahamas: Dept. of Archives.

Braithwaite, Kamau. 1973. *Contradictory Omens: Cultural Diversity and Integration in the Caribbean.* Mona, Jamaica: University of the West Indies; Kingston, Jamaica: Savacou Publications.

Brodber, Erna. 1975. *A Study of Yards in the City of Kingston.* Institute of Social and Economic Research, Working Paper no. 9. University of the West Indies, Kingston, Jamaica.

Burnside, J.J. 1867. Report on Visit to Andros and Grand Bahama after 1866 Hurricane. Governor's Despatches. Hurricane 19 January. Bahamas National Archives document. In *A Guide to Selected Sources for the History of the Seminole Settlements at Red Bays, Andros, 1817–1980,* by David E. Wood, appendix 20, p. 16. Nassau, Bahamas: Department of Archives.

Carew, Jan. 1988. *Fulcrums of Change.* Trenton, N.J.: Africa World Press.

———. 1992. United We Stand! Joint Struggles of Native American and African American in the Columbian Era. *Monthly Review* 44, no. 3 (July–August): 103.

Cash, Phillip, Shirley Gordon, and Gail Saunders. 1991. *Sources of Bahamian History.* London: Macmillan.

Clarke, Edith. 1957. *My Mother Who Fathered Me.* London: George Allen and Unwin.

Collinwood, Dean W. 1989a. *The Bahamas: Between Worlds.* Decatur: White Sound Press.

———. 1989b. The Bahamas in Social Transition. In *Modern Bahamian Society,* ed. Dean W. Collinwood and Steve Dodge, 3–26. Parkersburg, Iowa: Caribbean Books.

Commonwealth of the Bahamas. 1974. *Aspects of Slavery: A Booklet of the Exhibition of Historical Documents held at the Public Records Office, Mackey Street.* February 12–16. Ministry of Education and Culture. Nassau, Bahamas.

———. 1984. *Aspects of Slavery Part II: A Booklet to Commemorate the 150th Anniversary of the Abolition of Slavery.* Bahamas Department of Archives, Ministry of Education.

———. 1989. *The Bahamas in the Age of Revolution, 1775–1848.* Nassau, Bahamas: Department of Archives, Ministry of Education.

Conniff, Michael L., and Thomas J. Davis. 1994. *Africans in the Americas: A History of the Black Diaspora.* New York: St. Martin's Press.

Cox, Oliver C. 1971. Caste, Class, and Race. Quoted in *Race and Politics in the Bahamas,* by Colin P. Hughes, 72. New York: St. Martin's Press, 1981, 72.

Craton, Michael. 1982. *Testing the Chains: Resistance to Slavery in the British West Indies.* Ithaca: Cornell University Press.

Creel, Margaret W. 1988. *"A Peculiar People": Slave Religion and Community among the Gullahs.* New York: New York University Press.

Curtin, Philip D. 1994. From Guesses to Calculations. In *The Atlantic Slave Trade,* ed. David Northrup, 39–49. Lexington, Mass.: D. C. Heath.

Defries, Amelia D. 1929. *The Fortunate Islands: Being Adventures with the Negro in the Bahamas.* London: C. Palmer.

Deveaux, Earl D. 1997. *A Social and Economic Contract with the People of Andros.* Nassau, Bahamas: Media Publishing.

Dodge, Steve. 1989. Independence and Separatism. In *Modern Bahamian History,* ed. D. W. Collinwood and S. Dodge, 39–68. Parkersburg, Iowa: Caribbean Books.

Du Bois, W.E.B. 1962 [1935]. *Black Reconstruction in America, 1860–1880: An Essay toward a History of the Part Which Black Folk Played in the Attempt to Reconstruct Democracy in America.* Studies in American Negro Life, A. Meier, general editor. New York: Atheneum.

Edelman, Murray J. 1972. *The Symbolic Uses of Politics.* Urbana: University of Illinois Press.

Edie, Carlene J. 1991. *Democracy by Default.* Boulder: Lynne Riemer.

Feagin, Joe R., and Clairece B. Feagin. 1999. *Racial and Ethnic Relations.* Upper Saddle River, N.J.: Prentice Hall.

Finnegan, Ruth H. 1992. *Oral Traditions and the Verbal Arts: A Guide to Research Practices.* London: Routledge Press.

Flagg, Harold. 2000. Black Indians of Red Bays. In *Bahamas Handbook.* Nassau, Bahamas: Etienne Dupuch, Jr., Publications.

Forbes, Jack D. 1993. *Africans and Native Americans: The Language of Race and the Evolution of Red-Black Peoples.* Urbana: University of Illinois Press.

Foster, Laurence. 1935. Negro-Indian Relationships in the Southeast. Ph.D. diss., University of Pennsylvania.

Franco, José L. 1968. Cuatro siglos de kucha por la libertad: los palenques. In *La Presencia Negra en el Nuevo Mundo,* 91–135. Havana: Casa de las Americas.

Frazier, Edward F. 1966 [1939]. *The Negro Family in the United States.* Chicago: University of Chicago Press.

Free National Movement. 1997. *Manifesto II: Agenda to and for the Twenty-first Century.* Nassau, Bahamas: Free National Movement.

Geertz, Clifford. 1973. *The Interpretation of Cultures.* New York: Basic Books.

Giddings, Joshua R. 1858. *The Exiles of Florida: or, The Crimes Committed by Our Government against the Maroons, Who Fled from South Carolina and Other Slave States, Seeking Protection under Spanish Laws*. Columbus: Follett, Foster.

Goggin, John M. 1937. Bahama Journal. P. K. Yonge Collection, University of Florida.

———. 1946. The Seminole Negroes of Andros Island, Bahamas. *Florida Historical Quarterly* 24: 201–6.

Gonzalez, Nancy L. 1984. Rethinking the Consanguineal Household and Matrifocality. *Ethnology* 23: 1–12.

Governor's Desptaches 1827–1831. Bahamas. Department of Archives.

Grant, Sir Lewis. 1821. CO23/70/5 (April 19, 1821). Microfilm. Nassau, Bahamas: Bahamas Department of Archives.

———. 1828. CO23/78/58 (June 30, 1828). Microfilm. Nassau, Bahamas: Bahamas Department of Archives.

Guillot, Carlos F. 1961. *Negros rebeldes y negros cimarrones: Perfil afro-americano en la historia del Nuevo Mundo durante el siglo XVI*. Montevideo: Farina Editores.

Guthrie, Patricia. 1996. *Catching Sense: African American Communities on a South Carolina Sea Island*. Westport, Conn.: Bergin and Garvey.

Hall, Stuart. 1996. Introduction: Who Needs Identity? In *Questions of Cultural Identity*, ed. Stuart Hall and Paul DuGay, 1–10. London: Sage Publications.

Hall, Stuart, and Paul DuGay, eds. 1996. *Questions of Cultural Identity*. London: Sage Publications.

Harris, Marvin. 1964. *Patterns of Race in the Americas*. Westport, Conn.: Greenwood Press.

Harrison, Faye V. 1995. The Persistent Power of "Race" in the Cultural and Political Economy of Racism. *Annual Review of Anthropology* 24: 47–74.

Harrison, Faye V., ed. 1991. *Decolonizing Anthropology: Moving Further toward an Anthropology for Liberation*. Arlington, Va.: American Anthropological Association.

Harrison, Ira E., and Faye V. Harrison. 1999. *African-American Pioneers in Anthropology*. Urbana: University of Illinois Press.

Herron, Jordan T. 1994. The Black Seminole Settlement Pattern, 1813–1842. Master's thesis, University of South Carolina.

Herskovits, Melville J. 1958 [1941]. *The Myth of the Negro Past*. Boston: Beacon Press.

———. 1938. *Acculturation: The Study of Culture Contact*. New York: J. J. Augustin.

Higginbotham, A. Leon, Jr. 1978. *In The Matter Of Color: Race and the American Legal Process*. Oxford: Oxford University Press.

Hill, Jonathan D. 1996. Introduction: Ethnogenesis in the Americas, 1492–1992. In *History, Power, and Identity: Ethnogenesis in the Americas, 1492–1992*, ed. Jonathan D. Hill. Iowa City: University of Iowa Press.

Hudson, Charles M., ed. 1971. *Red, White, and Black: Symposium on Indians in the Old South*. Athens: University of Georgia Press.

Hughes, Colin P. 1981. *Race and Politics in the Bahamas*. New York: St. Martin's Press.

———. 1989. Symbolic Politics in a Racially Divided Society. In *Modern Bahamian Society*, ed. Dean W. Collinwood and Steve Dodge, 69–92. Parkersburg, Iowa: Caribbean Books.

Hursh, Cyndi. n.d. Andros Island. Unpublished manuscript.

Hurston, Zora Neale. 1942. *Dust Tracks on a Road*. New York: Harper Perennial.

Johnson, Howard. 1991. *The Bahamas in Slavery and Freedom*. Kingston, Jamaica: Ian Randle Publishers; London: James Currey Publishers.

Joyner, Charles. 1984. *Down by the Riverside: A South Carolina Slave Community*. Urbana: University of Illinois Press.

Katz, William L. 1986. *Black Indians: A Hidden Heritage*. New York: Atheneum.

Kersey, Harry A., Jr. 1987. *The Seminole and Miccosukee Tribes: A Critical Biography*. Bloomington: Indiana University Press.

Klos, George. 1989. Blacks and the Seminole Removal Debate, 1821–1835. *Florida Historical Quarterly* 68: 55–78.

Knight, Franklin W., ed. 1997. *General History of the Caribbean*. Vol. 3, *The Slave Societies of the Caribbean*. London: UNESCO Publishing/Macmillan Education.

LaFlamme, Alan G. 1985. *Green Turtle Cay: An Island in the Bahamas*. Prospect Heights, Ill.: Waveland Press.

Landers, Jane L. 1996. *Against the Odds: Free Blacks in the Slave Societies of the Americas*. London: Frank Cass.

———. 1995. Traditions of African American Freedom and Community in Spanish Colonial Florida. In *The African American Heritage of Florida*, ed. David R. Colburn and Jane L. Landers. Gainesville: University Press of Florida.

Layder, Derek. 1994. *Understanding Social Theory*. London: Sage Publications.

Leach, Edmund R. 1961. *Rethinking Anthropology*. New York: Athlone Press.

Littlefield, Daniel. 1977. *Africans and Seminoles from Removal to Emancipation*. Westport, Conn.: Greenwood Press.

———. 1981. *Rice and Slaves: Ethnicity and the Slave Trade in Colonial South Carolina*. Baton Rouge: Louisiana State University Press.

Logan, G. 1969. Bahamian Pride of Heritage Could Be Example for Some. *Miami Herald*, February 20.

MacCormack, Carol P., and A. Draper. 1987. *Social and Cognitive Aspects of Female Sexuality in Jamaica*. London: Academic Press.

Magnarella, Paul J. 1991. *Human Materialism: A Model of Sociocultural Systems and a Strategy for Analysis*. Gainesville: University Press of Florida.

Maingot, Anthony P. 1994. *The United States and the Caribbean*. Warwick University Caribbean Studies. London: Macmillan.

Manwaring, George Ernest. 1957 [1928]. *Woodes Rogers: Privateer and Governor*. London: Cassell.

Massiah, Joycelin. 1986. Caribbean Women and Familial Experiences. *Social and Economic Studies* 55, no. 2: 1–30.

McCall, George Archibald. 1974 [1868]. *Letters from the Frontiers.* Facsimile reproduction. Gainesville: University Press of Florida.

McClaurin, Irma. 1996. *Women of Belize: Gender and Change in Central America.* New Brunswick, N.J.: Rutgers University Press.

McKenzie, H. 1993. *The Family, Class and Ethnicity in the Future of the Caribbean.* Mona, Jamaica: University of the West Indies.

Mead, Margaret, and Rhoda Métraux. 1953. *The Study of Culture at a Distance.* Chicago: University of Chicago Press.

Miller, S. A. 1997. Wild Cat's Bones: Seminole Leadership in a Seminole Cosmos. Ph.D. diss., University of Nebraska.

Mintz, S. E. 1985. *Sweetness and Power.* New York: Viking.

Moore, John H. 1996. Mvskoke Personal Names. *Names* 43, no. 3: 187–212.

Moseley, Mary. 1926. *The Bahamas Handbook.* Nassau, Bahamas: Nassau Guardian.

Mulroy, Kevin. 1993. *Freedom on the Border: The Seminole Maroons in Florida, the Indian Territory, Coahuila, and Texas.* Lubbock: Texas Tech University Press.

Munnings, William V. 1819. Governor's Despatches 1818–1825. In *A Guide to Selected Sources for the History of the Seminole Settlements at Red Bays, Andros, 1817–1980,* by D. E. Wood, appendix 5 (September 30). Nassau, Bahamas: Department of Archives.

Mykel, Nancy. 1962. *The Seminole Towns—A Compilation Prepared for Sociology 630 under Dr. John M. Goggin.* Gainesville: University of Florida.

Nassau Magazine. 1958. Andros the Fabled Island of the Bahamas. Vol. 11, no. 1 (autumn). Ref. #27, Bahamas Department of Archives.

———. 1938. The Story of Robert Armbrister: The Honorable P. W. D. Armbrister, O.B.E. Vol. 5, no. 3 (February). Ref. #16, Bahamas Department of Archives.

Neill, Wilfred T. 1952. Florida's Seminole Indians. *Florida Anthropologist* (January).

Nettleford, Rex. 1970. *Mirror, Mirror: Identity, Race, and Protest in Jamaica.* New York: Morrow.

Newton, Bertram A. 1968. *A History of Red Bays, Andros, Bahamas.* Red Bays, Bahamas: Bertram A. Newton.

Northrop, A. R. 1910. Bahaman Trip, General Notes. In *Bahaman Trip, General Notes,* ed. John I. Northrop and Henry F. Osborn. New York: Columbia University Press.

Otterbein, Keith F. 1963. *The Family Organization of the Andros Islanders: A Case Study of the Mating System and Household Composition of a Community in the Bahama Islands.* Ph.D. diss., University of Pittsburgh.

Page, Helan. 1993. Teaching Comparative Social Order and Caribbean Social Change. In *Spirit, Space and Survival,* ed. J. James and R. Farmer, 63–82. New York: Routledge Press.

Paranjpe, Anand C., ed. 1986. *Ethnic Identities and Prejudices: Perspectives from the Third World.* Leiden, Netherlands: E. J. Brill.

Parsons, Elsie C. 1918. *Folk-Tales of Andros Island, Bahamas.* Cambridge, Mass.: American Folklore Society.

Payne, Anthony. 1993. *Westminster Adapted: The Political Order of the Commonwealth Caribbean.* Baltimore: Johns Hopkins University Press.

Peggs, Deans. 1957 [1928]. *Woodes Rogers: Privateer and Governour.* London: Cassell (first publisher); Margate, Kent, Eng.: Thanet Press (reprinting).

Pocock, John G. A. 1971. *Politics, Language, and Time: Essays in Political Thought and History.* New York: Atheneum.

Porter, Kenneth W. 1971. *The Negro on the American Frontier.* New York: Arno Press, New York Times Collection.

———. 1996. *The Black Seminoles: History of a Freedom-Seeking People.* Gainesville: University Press of Florida.

———. 1945. Notes on Seminole Negroes in the Bahamas. *Florida Historical Quarterly* 24: 56–60.

Potter, Woodburne. 1836. The War in Florida. Readex Microprint. 1966.

Price, Richard, ed. 1979. *Maroon Societies: Rebel Slave Communities in the Americas.* Baltimore: Johns Hopkins University Press.

Ramos, Guerreiro. 1957. *Introducao Critica Sociologia Brasileira.* Rio de Janeiro: Editora Andes.

Ramsaran, Ramesh. 1989. *The Bahamas: An Assessment of Post-Independence Economic Experience.* Parkersburg, Iowa: Caribbean Books.

Randolph, Logan R. 1994. *An Ethnobiological Investigation of Andros Island, Bahamas.* Ph.D. diss. Miami University.

Ranger, Terence O. 1988. *Chingaira Makoni's Head: Myth, History, and the Colonial Experience.* Bloomington, Ind.: African Studies Program, Indiana University.

Rawnsley, David. 1961. Legend of the Chickcharnies. *Nassau Magazine* (spring). Ref. 25. Bahamas Department of Archives.

Richardson, M. D. n.d. *Negro History in Florida: Federal Writer's Project 1939–1941.* Jacksonville: s.n.

Robinson, Donald. 1971. *Slavery in the Structure of American Politics.* New York: W. W. Norton.

Safa, Helen I. 1986. Economic Autonomy and Sexual Equality in Caribbean Society. *Social and Economic Research* 35: 1–19.

———, 1995. *The Myth of the Male Breadwinner.* Boulder: Westview Press.

———. 1998. Race and Nationality in the Americas: Introduction. *Latin American Perspectives* 25, no. 3: 3–20.

Saunders, Gail. 1983. *Bahamian Loyalists and their Slaves.* London: Macmillan Education.

———. 1994 [1990]. *Bahamian Society after Emancipation.* Kingston, Jamaica: Ian Randle Publishers.

———. 1993. The General Strike in Nassau: A Landmark in Bahamian History. *Journal of Caribbean History* 27, no. 1: 81–113.

———. 1985. *Slavery in the Bahamas, 1648–1838.* Nassau, Bahamas: Nassau Guardian.

Schneider, David M. 1980 [1968]. *American Kinship: A Cultural Account.* Chicago: University of Chicago Press.

———. 1984. *A Critique of the Study of Kinship.* Ann Arbor: University of Michigan Press.

Schusky, Ernest L. 1983. *Manual for Kinship Analysis.* Lanham, Md.: University Press of America.

Shaw, Carolyn M. 1995. *Colonial Inscriptions: Race, Sex, and Class in Kenya.* Minneapolis: University of Minnesota Press.

Simey, Thomas S. 1946. *Welfare and Planning in the West Indies.* Oxford: Clarendon Press.

Simmons, William H. 1973 [1822]. *Notices of East Florida.* Gainesville: University Press of Florida.

Sithole, Musaemura. 1986. *The Salience of Ethnicity in African Politics: The Case of Zimbabwe.* Leiden, Netherlands: E. J. Brill.

Slave Registers 1821–1834. Bahamas Department of Archives.

Smith, Raymond T. 1988. *Kinship and Class in the West Indies.* Cambridge: Cambridge University Press.

Smyth, James C. 1831. August 10. London Duplicate Despatches. In *A Guide to Selected Sources for the History of the Seminole Settlements at Red Bays, Andros, 1817–1980,* by D. E. Wood, appendix 13 (August 10). Nassau, Bahamas: Department of Archives.

Sturtevant, William. 1971. Creek into Seminole. In *North American Indians in Historical Perspective,* ed. E. B. Leacock and N. O. Lurie, 92–128. New York: Random House.

Swanton, John Reed. 1998 [1922]. *Early History of the Creek Indians and Their Neighbors.* Gainesville: University Press of Florida.

———. 1953. *Indian Tribes of North America.* Bulletin 145. Washington, D.C.: Bureau of American Ethnology.

———. 1946. *The Indians of the Southeastern United States.* Washington, D.C.: United States Government Printing Office.

Twining, Mary A., and Keith E. Baird, eds. 1991. *Sea Island Roots: African Presence in the Carolinas and Georgia.* Trenton, N.J.: Africa World Press.

Van Sertima, Ivan. 1976. *They Came before Columbus: The African Presence in Ancient America.* New York: Random House.

Vansina, Jan. 1985. *Oral Tradition as History.* London: James Currey.

Weik, Terrance. In press. Freedom Fighters on the Florida Frontier: Black Seminole

Maroons at Abraham's Old Town. In *Unlocking the Past: Historical Archaeology in North America*. Gainesville: Society for Historical Archaeology and the University Press of Florida.

Weisman, Brent R. 2000. The Plantation System of the Florida Seminole Indians and Black Seminoles during the Colonial Era. In *Colonial Plantations and Economy in Florida*, ed. Jane L. Landers. Gainesville: University Press of Florida.

———. 1989. *Like Beads on a String: A Culture History of the Seminole Indians in Northern Peninsular Florida*. Tuscaloosa: University of Alabama Press.

Whitehead, Tony L. 1980. Identity, Subjectivity, and Cultural Bias in Fieldwork. *The Black Scholar*, September–October.

Williams, Eric. 1944. *Capitalism and Slavery*. Chapel Hill: University of North Carolina Press.

Williams, Walter L., ed. 1979. *Southeastern Indians: Since the Removal Era*. Athens: University of Georgia Press.

Wilson, Franklyn R. 1989. Bahamianization and Economic Development. In *Modern Bahamian Society*, ed. Dean W. Collinwood and Steve Dodge, 139–49. Parkersburg, Iowa: Caribbean Books.

Windley, Lathan A. 1983. *Runaway Slave Advertisements: A Documentary History from the 1730s to 1790*. Vol. 4, *Georgia*. Westport, Conn.: Greenwood Press.

Wood, David E. 1990. Free People of Colour in Nineteenth-Century Bahamian Society. *Journal of the Bahamas Historical Society* 12, no. 1.

———. 1980. *A Guide to Selected Sources for the History of the Seminole Settlements at Red Bays, Andros 1817–1980*. Nassau, Bahamas: Department of Archives.

Woodson, Carter G. 1920. The Relations of Negroes and Indians in Massachusetts. *Journal of Negro History* 5: 44–57.

Wright, James L., Jr. 1976. Blacks in British East Florida. *Florida Historical Quarterly*. April. Tampa: Florida Historical Society.

———. 1986. *Creeks and Seminoles: The Destruction and Regeneration of the Muscogulge People*. Lincoln: University of Nebraska Press.

Young, Virginia H. 1993. *Becoming West Indian: Culture, Self, and Nation in St. Vincent*. Washington, D.C.: Smithsonian Institution Press.

Zinn, Howard. 1980. *A People's History of the United States*. New York: HarperCollins.

Index

Rosalyn Howard is assistant professor of anthropology at the University of Central Florida.

www.ingramcontent.com/pod-product-compliance
Lightning Source LLC
Chambersburg PA
CBHW020549270326
41927CB00006B/777